MW01707483

American Probate

American Probate

▼

Protecting the **Public**
Improving the **Process**

Paula A. Monopoli

Northeastern University Press
Boston

Northeastern University Press

Copyright 2003 by Paula A. Monopoli

All rights reserved. Except for the quotation of short passages for the purposes of criticism and review, no part of this book may be reproduced in any form or by any means, electronic or mechanical, including photocopying, recording, or any information storage and retrieval system now known or to be invented, without written permission of the publisher.

Library of Congress Cataloging-in-Publication Data

Monopoli, Paula A., 1958–
American probate : protecting the public, improving the process / Paula A. Monopoli.
p. cm.
Includes bibliographical references and index.
ISBN 1–55553–572-0 (cloth : acid-free paper)
1. Probate law and practice—United States. I. Title.
KF765 .M66 2003
346.7305′2—dc21 2002154299

Designed by Janis Owens

Composed in New Aster by Coghill Composition Company in Richmond, Virginia. Printed and bound by The Maple Press in York, Pennsylvania. The paper is Sebago Antique, an acid-free sheet.

MANUFACTURED IN THE UNITED STATES OF AMERICA
07 06 05 04 03 5 4 3 2 1

For Marin, Richard, Victoria,

Christopher, Patrick, Mom and Dad

▼

Contents

▼

Preface

▼

Following the tragic events of September 11, 2001, Americans rushed to their lawyers' offices to sign wills. As one estate planning attorney said, "September 11 took away the ability to do what people do when they come in to talk about wills, which is to say, 'Here's what I'd like to do if I die'—as if they have a choice. . . . Now it's not if but when."[1] Except for the recent phase-out of the federal estate tax, little public attention has been paid to the process by which we pass wealth from one generation to the next. As the following chapters demonstrate, that process may be seriously flawed.

Most Americans give little thought to the legal ramifications of death. Some people may go to court only once in their lives, to probate a loved one's will or to become the guardian of an elderly relative. Their experience in probate court may have a profound effect on their view of the American legal system. How lawyers conduct themselves, and whether probate courts work well, may make the difference between a public that values the American legal profession and one that reviles it.

Lawyers involved in the process called "probate" are at the heart of the stories that follow. These cases illustrate a process that allowed lawyers to breach the trust reposed in them by the elderly and those otherwise incapable of caring for their own interests. There is an old adage that a society is measured by how it treats its most vulnerable members. The most vulnerable clients are those who cannot monitor their legal representatives—incompetent wards whose court-appointed guardians are supposed to manage their money to provide for their care, or decedents who trusted a lawyer/executor to distribute their estates.

The structure of American probate has led to abuses over the years. In response, there has been a movement toward transferring wealth through "nonprobate" devices. There also has been an important reform movement in the law, embodied in the Uniform Probate Code and the new Uniform Trust Code, toward a more passive view of the probate court's role. The increasing use of nonprobate transfers of wealth and the conceptual shift toward a "bystander" model of the probate court are positive developments. Yet they may warrant reevaluation in some circumstances, for example, when lawyers draft instruments that name them as fiduciaries. Passive probate works well for sophisticated consumers of probate services. But it is not without costs for the unsophisticated consumer who lacks the resources to access information and monitor the players in the probate process. Considering the tendency of human beings to be tempted by large amounts of money, less savvy participants in the American probate system often suffer.

Reform is possible, and, with a commitment on the part of the public to better fund its courts, even probable. This book offers a tripartite blueprint for reform: increasing deterrence, detection, and compensation in the American probate system. The revolution in information technology makes successfully implementing this blueprint more likely than at any prior time in our nation's history. America's lawyers and judges have the tools to improve the system. Whether they use those tools is up to them.

Acknowledgments

▼

My first experience with the American probate process was in 1982, when my father died suddenly during my second year of law school. I flew home to Massachusetts to help my mother, who was left alone with four young children. We consulted a local lawyer who proposed that he receive 10 percent of my father's assets in exchange for probating the estate. I thought the fee high and thought my mother and siblings, Beth, Chris, Rich, and Dan, more deserving recipients of the 10 percent. My mother and I decided to save the lawyer's fee by doing the work ourselves. We owe much to family and friends, including some who were familiar with probate, who helped us through that time and through that process.

My editors at Northeastern University Press, Bill Frohlich and Emily McKeigue, and Bill's assistant, Sarah Rowley, have helped move this project forward. My research assistants over the years, Christy Pritts, Initia Lettau, Rob Burriesci, Michelle Pirozzi, Diana Danmeyer, Kate Meehan, Chris Schmidt, and Sara Turner, deserve special recognition, as does my administrative assistant, Michael Cuneo. Discussions with my colleagues at the University of Maryland School of Law, including Jana Singer, Richard Boldt, and David Hyman, sharpened many of the ideas in this book. David English and members of the Joint Editorial Board for the Uniform Trusts & Estates Acts, including John Langbein, Edward Halbach, Eugene Scoles, and Mary Louise Fellows, influenced my ideas through their comments at the February 2002 symposium on the new Uniform Trust Code. Lawyers, judges, and others, including John Maher, Sharon Miller, Pete Kennedy, John Westover, Harry Westover, and Richard Mottola were willing to share their time, experiences, and insights.

This book is dedicated to my family and to the memory of my father, Richard Monopoli. I am very grateful to my husband, Marin Scordato, and to my children, Richard, Victoria, Christopher, and Patrick, for being willing to sacrifice time with me while I worked on this manuscript. Finally, I owe many thanks to my mother, Eileen Monopoli, without whose constant support, editorial assistance, and encouragement this book never would have been completed.

American Probate

Chapter 1

The Purposes of Probate

▼

On a March day in 1994, at the MGM Grand in Las Vegas, hotel security knocked on the door to Room 21312. The room's occupant had registered as Richard Mansfield of Quebec, Canada. When he missed his checkout time by a full day and had not shown up at the hotel desk to pay for an additional night, security came knocking. Inside they found the body of a seventy-year-old man, lying dead on the bed with a plastic bag over his head. A suicide note taped to the mirror indicated that the man was not Richard Mansfield, but a fugitive New Hampshire judge named John Fairbanks.[1]

John Fairbanks' troubles had begun years before in the small New Hampshire town of Newport. In 1973, a new probate judge, Jarlath Slattery, was appointed in Sullivan County. He was unnerved to find the small-town probate court in disarray—twelve years of dusty estate papers relating to guardianships, trusts, and estates lay unfiled in the dingy probate court vault.[2] There was no indexing, no system, no way for the Sullivan County Register of Probate, Bernice A. MacWilliams, to keep track of the cases filed in her court. The new probate judge ordered the chaos cleaned up, but the cozy, small-town atmosphere of the court continued to aid Fairbanks in shielding his unethical behavior as the executor and trustee for a number of trusting clients.

John Fairbanks was a pillar of his community. He was Bernice MacWilliams' lawyer.[3] He was also a part-time district court judge. Fairbanks had been an active member of the bar for more than forty years, and a district court judge for more than thirty.[4] During those years, he had handled many probate matters and was appointed executor or trustee of dozens of estates.

One of the estates John Fairbanks handled was that of Diane Trudeau's father. By 1976, Ms. Trudeau began to feel that something was amiss. She took her complaints to the proper place, the New Hampshire Supreme Court's Professional Conduct Committee, which oversees the conduct of New Hampshire's 3,600-plus lawyers. Diane Trudeau expected justice, but justice was not to be. After reviewing the complaint, the committee—of which John Fairbanks was a member—found nothing inappropriate in its colleague's behavior and closed the matter.[5] Trudeau's effort to expose Fairbanks, which would have saved dozens of clients from his theft in subsequent years, was to no avail. Her allegation that Fairbanks sold property belonging to her father's estate to one of his own business partners, and that he had not recorded any deeds in the names of the heirs who were supposed to receive the property, died a quiet death, buried in bureaucracy.

In 1977, as Trudeau was trying to expose Fairbanks, the citizens of Sullivan County reelected octogenarian and nursing home resident Bernice MacWilliams as the Sullivan County Register of Probate, continuing her tenure of more than thirty-five years in the post.[6]

In her later years, MacWilliams only went to her office at the probate court "occasionally, for just a few hours at a time,"[7] until she finally retired in 1981. John Fairbanks continued to add clients to his busy practice, and on August 7, 1982, he took on the guardianship of Richard Tweedy, whose brother John was to prove to be one of Fairbanks' most vocal critics in the years to come.

In addition to electing probate registers, who are constitutional officers, New Hampshire is somewhat unique in having part-time judicial appointments.[8] Not only was John Fairbanks an active probate attorney, he was a part-time district court judge in Sullivan County hearing criminal matters. He often appeared as a probate attorney before his colleague Harry Spanos, one of the two Sullivan County probate judges. This cozy state of affairs was later the object of legislative criticism and a reprimand of Judge Spanos, but in 1982 things were running as they always had in Sullivan County.

Except for a brief letter in January 1983 to the New Hampshire attorney general's office warning that Fairbanks had forgotten to notify the director of the George W. Paul Trust of a sale of stock, John Fairbanks continued to hum along, enjoying his home in Newport and a beautiful house in the ocean-front community of Ogunquit, Maine. It was not until September 1987 that a second formal complaint was filed against John Fairbanks with the Professional Conduct Committee, this time by Prentice Coonley-Demers, regarding her mother's estate. Fairbanks was removed as guardian of the estate, and he paid $41,000 to settle the matter.[9] But again, the matter stopped there—no investigation or charges followed.

The Meding Trust

▼

It was during these years that John Fairbanks was named Helen Meding's executor. Meding was Fairbanks' client. In January 1985, Fairbanks asked another law firm to prepare a new will and some new trust documents for Meding. She executed new estate planning papers on January 21, 1985 and died five days later. Fairbanks was appointed executor of Meding's estate on February 19, 1985. New Hampshire law required him to submit an inventory of the estate's assets within ninety days of his appointment. Fairbanks did not come close. The inventory was filed at the probate court more than one year later, on May 6, 1986.[10]

Though Fairbanks failed to get his inventory done in time, he did write to the Dartmouth National Bank—the bank that was the trustee of Helen Meding's Trust—to demand $265,000 for estate taxes, administrative expenses, and debts of the Meding estate and for funds to cover funeral expenses. The bank wrote a check for the full amount on November 25, 1985, without asking for a breakdown of expenses or taking even the most basic precautions against improper handling of the money by making the check payable to the Internal Revenue Service. The bank simply sent the check to John Fairbanks.[11]

Fairbanks kept missing deadlines. New Hampshire law required a detailed accounting in court one year after his appointment as executor. He missed that deadline too, failing to file the account until September 24, 1987—more than six months late. The probate court did not sanction him. By this point, Fairbanks was clearly dipping into the Meding estate funds, and he failed to record in the probate court accounting the large $265,000 transfer received from the trust.[12] He did not file another account until December 12, 1988, and the final account "was the same as the first."[13]

Helen Meding's children, Stephen Meding and Virginia Keach, grew suspicious. They kept pushing the bank trust officer, Janice Milne, to allow them access to the trust principal and to split the trust, actions that could only be done when the estate had been closed. In 1987, they began to complain to Milne about Fairbanks' tardiness and his failure to return phone calls. Milne wrote to Fairbanks on June 15, 1987, "We're waiting for a copy [of the estate tax closing letter] so we can go ahead and split the trust for Ginny and Steve's benefit."[14] Fairbanks did not reply. Though they had no response, the bank reassured Helen Meding's children that all was in order. In fact, Fairbanks had stolen the money. The taxes never were paid.

Finally, Janice Milne decided to go directly to the probate court. On January 15, 1988, she had a trust department secretary write to the Merrimack County Probate Court to obtain copies of the inventory and accounts.[15] The bank apparently did not read them closely enough to note that the $265,000 transfer was not reported.

In April 1988, Prentice Coonley, a friend of Stephen Meding, warned Meding that Fairbanks had mishandled her financial affairs. Meding passed this warning on to the bank, but it did nothing. Fairbanks filed his final account in December 1988 and sent the bank a check for $7,506.15.[16]

It was not until September 1989, nine months later, that the attorney general's office contacted Helen Meding's beneficiaries about Fairbanks' suspected misconduct. The beneficiaries went to the probate court and obtained the documents themselves. Fairbanks' theft was obvious. As one judge put it, "There appears little doubt that Fairbanks, as executor, stole significant assets from the Meding Trust."[17]

Helen Meding's estate was worth $1,108,459. The taxes, if paid, would have been $261,935.25. Had the theft not occurred, Stephen

Meding, Virginia Keach, and Helen Meding's other beneficiaries would have enjoyed the remaining $846,523.75. After John Fairbanks was done, the estate was worth only $674,545.19. The estate paid taxes of $177,570.54, and only $496,974.65 remained for Meding's five beneficiaries. Fairbanks had stolen the difference—$349,549.10.[18]

The Initial Investigation

▼

While Fairbanks handled Helen Meding's estate, he was also acting as guardian for John Tweedy's retarded brother, Richard. While Meding beneficiaries were asking questions about Fairbanks' tardiness in their mother's estate filings, John Tweedy was filing a second complaint against Fairbanks with the Professional Conduct Committee. He followed this up in December 1988 with a request to the New Hampshire attorney general's office to investigate Fairbanks' handling of his brother's estate. Tweedy's statement laid out his efforts to force Fairbanks to make an accounting of his brother's estate, efforts that had been met with the same stonewalling the Medings experienced. Fairbanks had failed to file accounts and reports since 1975,[19] with no apparent sanction by the probate court, which is not surprising given the chaotic state of the register's files.

On January 4, 1989, investigators from the attorney general's office gave the Tweedy complaint to the Sullivan County Probate Court.[20]

That spring, rumors of Fairbanks' wrongdoing began to travel in the close-knit legal community of Sullivan County. Peter Burling, a local attorney and state representative, began "to hear that something [was] really wrong . . . [and that] something [was] going on in the Registry of Probate."[21] Finally, after three complaints in twelve years, the Professional Conduct Committee of the New Hampshire Supreme Court appointed Attorney Arthur Nighswander to look into Fairbanks' files and the operation of the Sullivan County Probate Court. Nighswander and CPA Dale Plavnicky, the internal auditor for the State Supreme Court, reviewed Fairbanks' files (the more than 100 cases he had handled since 1978, either as attorney or fiduciary). Nighswander reported to the court in August, concluding: "The pattern seems clear going back to 1978, 1979, and 1980 the inventories were almost always late, sometimes being filed along with the account . . . we found little evidence of any notice from the probate court to him [Fairbanks] or to the fiduciary he represented saying there was any delinquency. . . . [t]here seemed to be no system by which the Register would be aware of the delinquency when it happened and if so any notices were probably oral, depending upon the Fiduciary or the Attorney to take care of the matter."[22]

Nighswander highlighted the fact that the two part-time probate judges paid little attention to procedure unless a complaint was filed or the register brought a problem to their attention. Nighswander captured the essence of the Sullivan County Probate Court when he said, "It is my understanding that [Mrs. MacWilliams] was very political. She knew the people of influence, and the ones to whom favor should be given, and she ran the Registry of Probate on a very personal basis. As far as I know, there is no record in the files. . . . Most everything was done on a personal basis by telephone or by personal conversation."[23]

Part-time judges with active practices were not unusual in New Hampshire. The Nighswander report pointed out that in this incestuous world, judges were likely to take the word of a colleague. There was no reason to disbelieve lawyers; you gave your friends the benefit of the doubt. When asked, Judge Spanos denied that he gave Fairbanks any special treatment. He could recall only one time when a lawyer was cited for contempt for failing to file an inventory or account. His comments capture the essence of the cozy world of the Sullivan County Probate Court. "Once in a while the Register would make up a list of inventories and accounts that were overdue and sent this list to John Fairbanks."[24] No formal notices, no threats of contempt for failing to file ever were issued, just a nice note from one colleague to another. The Nighswander report noted that "no notices were ever sent to the bonding company,"[25] even when Fairbanks failed to comply with the informal notice system that prevailed in the courthouse.

In another case, Judge Harry Spanos' brother Charles took on the task of trying to recover the assets of a former Fairbanks' client, Kaarle Lehtinen. Lehtinen had entrusted Judge Fairbanks with

$250,000 over ten years. The money seemed to have disappeared, and Lehtinen hired Charles Spanos to recover it. In April 1989, Spanos confronted Fairbanks in his Newport office and demanded a full accounting. Fairbanks promised to comply, but the subsequent account showed only $159,958.22 of Lehtinen's money in Fairbanks' possession.[26]

At about the same time, the attorney general's office sent a message to its investigators arguably aimed at blunting efforts to unmask John Fairbanks. "Before you do too much digging, you should interview Fairbanks and see if he has answers to Tweedy's questions. If he does, that should end the matter." The investigator replied to the assistant attorney general in charge of the case that, "on the surface, I don't think Fairbanks is guilty of anything more than lousy management, especially failing to make annual reports as required by law. . . . I feel that we should just interview Fairbanks and resolve the matter."[27] To some of Fairbanks' victims, that laissez-faire attitude seemed to indicate that the legal system was determined to protect its own. The subsequent legislative investigations criticized the attorney general's office for its performance in the Fairbanks case.

The Noose Finally Tightens

▼

As the criminal investigation stalled, Fairbanks' victims began to seek justice in civil court. In May 1989, realizing that the handwriting was on the wall, Fairbanks met with his lawyers, Jack Middleton and Robert Wells, in Manchester. He hired them to help close his law practice and to defend the suits being brought against him by his former clients in Sullivan County. There also was trouble brewing with the New Hampshire Supreme Court's Professional Conduct Committee, and he needed someone to help him avoid the possibility that his creditor/victims would proceed against him in U.S. Bankruptcy Court. Fairbanks also hired criminal expert Paul Barbadoro to work the criminal case that might be coming out of the attorney general's office and the county attorney's office.[28]

Under the growing weight of the negative publicity, John Fairbanks resigned after more than thirty years on the New Hampshire bench. He also resigned from the New Hampshire state bar, after more than forty years of practice, on June 6, 1989. Later that month, Sullivan County Attorney Mark Hathaway announced that he was convinced there was sufficient evidence to convene a grand jury to investigate John Fairbanks' activities as a lawyer and a fiduciary.[29]

In August 1989, the New Hampshire Supreme Court finally acted to protect the public from Fairbanks. Its members suspended Fairbanks from the practice of law, and he retreated to the seclusion of his $600,000 vacation home in Ogunquit.[30] That same month, the attorney general's investigator reported that former Fairbanks' clients had losses amounting to more than a million dollars. The victims challenged the findings, alleging that the attorney general's office had altered Fairbanks' documents in an effort to cover up his misdeeds and to protect him.[31]

As summer 1989 changed into a brilliant New England fall, the avalanche of complaints continued. More of Fairbanks' victims filed complaints with the New Hampshire Supreme Court's Professional Conduct Committee. Victims tried to get the attorney general's office to act on the Fairbanks case; in September, creditors filed a petition to reclaim their losses in U.S. Bankruptcy Court.[32]

In December 1989, Assistant Attorney General John Davis finally placed a call to Fairbanks' criminal lawyer, Paul Barbadoro. Fairbanks was about to be arrested and indicted for four class-A felonies involving the theft of $1.8 million. Would he rather surrender? In an exchange reminiscent of O. J. Simpson's lawyer, Robert Shapiro and the L.A. district attorney's office, Barbadoro agreed that his client would voluntarily appear the next day.[33] But like O. J. Simpson, Fairbanks was not about to cooperate. On the afternoon of December 28 Barbadoro informed the attorney general's office that he no longer had control of Fairbanks. County court personnel and state prosecutors sent an arrest warrant to police in Ogunquit. But Fairbanks had left hours before police knocked on his vacation home door. He noted in his diary on December 28: "JCF departs! Quebec City 5:15 (A.M.)."[34]

John Clough Fairbanks would never set foot in his home state of New Hampshire again.

The Purposes of Probate

As far back as 1623, the Inferior Court of Common Pleas adjudicated probate cases in New Hampshire.[35] Probate has always been an essential part of the legal system, and probate courts, when they run well, work to protect vulnerable members of society. However, the performance of the American probate court has often been less than stellar. Just what was the role of the court in which John Fairbanks was apparently given a license to steal?

The National College of Probate Court Judges is an organization dedicated to promoting efficient and effective probate courts. It characterizes the court's role as protective. "Probate courts are responsible for equitably handling many kinds of problems in our society. Though they deal primarily with the estates of deceased persons, probate courts also play a critical role in protecting the rights of people with special needs—the mentally ill, alcoholics, orphaned children, the aged, and developmentally disabled."[36] As the guardian of Richard Tweedy, John Tweedy's mentally disabled brother, Fairbanks was charged with protecting a disabled adult. As executor of Helen Meding's estate, he also played a protective role. He was supposed to marshal and preserve Meding's assets and distribute them to her trust. In both instances, John Fairbanks was acting as a fiduciary. The court granted him broad power necessary to fulfill his fiduciary obligations, but its failure to oversee the use of that power allowed things to go badly wrong.

The New Hampshire probate courts, like those of every other state, are judicial vehicles for "probating" the estates of deceased citizens. The term *probate* is derived from the Latin *probare,* which means to show or demonstrate.[37] Its canon law connection dates back to feudal England, where, "ecclesiastical courts controlled succession to personal property, which, before the time of the Tudors and the rise of

England as a trading power, was of little value (cows, sheep, utensils, personal ornaments, and such made up the personal property of medieval life)."[38] The king's common law courts handled the more valuable, and thus more important, asset, land. These courts, "gradually took over the administration of personal property. Ecclesiastical jurisdiction over decedents' estates was finally abolished in 1857, when a court of probate was established in chancery. However, the common law courts' jurisdiction over the succession to land continued. Not until 1925, with the Administration of Estates Act, was one English court given jurisdiction over succession to both real and personal property."[39]

The American colonies, later states, each developed their own methods of probating estates. The American probate courts lacked the religious underpinnings of the English ecclesiastical courts. The American system drew into a single court the cases that were spread among three different courts in England.[40] In some states, the early probate courts were courts of equity that grew into what are now called chancery, surrogate, or orphan's courts. In other states, judges in courts of general jurisdiction were given authority over probate matters. The result was a patchwork of approaches that even today varies among states, and sometimes among counties in a single state.[41] In New Hampshire, John Maher, the administrative judge appointed to bring professional management to the state's probate courts in the wake of the Fairbanks scandal, characterized the courts in the New Hampshire counties as "ten different fiefdoms."[42] The result of this autonomy is a lack of uniformity in procedures as well as in oversight.

In an effort to promote a uniform set of probate court standards, the National College of Probate Court Judges in 1993 embarked on a systematic study of the nation's probate courts. They noted that, "Although individual cases involving wills, decedents' estates, trusts, guardianships, and conservatorships—traditionally, matters within the jurisdiction of courts exercising probate jurisdiction—have garnered considerable public and professional attention, relatively little is known about the administration, operation, and performance of courts with probate jurisdiction."[43]

In response to the dearth of relevant research, the National College gathered its own data, documenting the organization of the American probate courts. They found that, as of 1990, there were forty-four states (including the District of Columbia) with judicial structures that included a court of "limited or special jurisdiction" over probate matters. These courts only handle a limited class of cases—for example, the probate of estates and the guardianships of incompetents. Within a given state, there can be as many as a thousand such courts.[44]

Twenty-one states and the District of Columbia have a formal probate court or division. Some of these states use the term "probate" to designate the court that handles these cases, while states like New Jersey and New York use the term "surrogate." Connecticut has statewide probate courts, organized into 133 separate probate court districts. Its probate court system is managed by a probate court administrator who oversees a staff that includes a chief counsel, a staff attorney; coordinators for administrative, social, and financial services; and technical and administrative support.[45]

A majority of states "have no formal probate court structure." For example, Arizona is one of thirty states where courts of general jurisdiction may have a probate department set up by local rule. Whether there is a separate court or not, there is wide variation in the jurisdiction of courts that handle matters loosely labeled "probate." The essential cases in a probate court's jurisdiction are wills, testamentary trusts, and decedents' estates. In the twenty states and the District of Columbia that have a formal probate court organization, the courts hear wills, trusts, and estate cases. Seventeen of these and the District of Columbia hear guardianship cases in these courts. In eleven of them and the District of Columbia, the courts also hear conservatorship cases.[46]

In addition to these basic duties, probate courts may hear cases as varied as involuntary civil commitment, adoptions, divorce, name changes, fish and game law violations, proceedings involving cemetery lots, and trusts related to community mausoleums.[47] But when average Americans think of probate, it is the wills, trusts and estate cases that come to mind, and the oversight of decedents' estates in particular.

The probate process is intended to perform several useful functions.[48] An executor is supposed to (1) collect or "marshal" all the decedent's assets and detail them on a list or "inventory"; (2) manage those assets during the several months or years it might take to administer the estate; (3) pay all those to whom the decedent owed debts, including hospital, doctor, and funeral bills and state and federal tax authorities; and (4) distribute what remains in the estate to the persons named in the will.[49]

These important functions are performed by a "personal representative," either an "executor" or "administrator." In the Fairbanks case, Helen Meding executed a will naming or "nominating" Fairbanks as her personal representative or executor.[50] Most probate courts oblige the decedent by making the person the decedent nominates the executor, but the court is not bound to do this. If someone objects, or if the court has misgivings about the nominee's ability to perform as a fiduciary, the court can name someone else. However, they rarely do.

If Helen Meding had died without a will, she would have died "intestate." In the event of intestacy, the probate court names an "administrator" rather than an "executor," usually a spouse, child or relative of the decedent. If there are no such relatives, then a lawyer or other court appointee will serve in this role. All fiduciaries must answer to the probate court, and judicial oversight is one of the major benefits the probate process offers. The requirement to account to the court is supposed to keep the personal representative honest in handling the decedent's cash, stocks and bonds, real estate, jewelry, and other valuable personal and real property.

Helen Meding also created a trust before her death. The Dartmouth National Bank was serving as trustee of this trust at Meding's death in January 1985.[51] Many Americans create such "inter vivos," "revocable," or "living" trusts in order to avoid the probate process altogether. Even when people have established trusts, however, any assets not funneled to the trust before the death of the person creating it must go through probate before making their way into the trust. As executor of Helen Meding's estate, John Fairbanks had unbridled power over Mrs. Meding's nontrust or "probate" assets and was charged with the duty of managing them, paying her debts and taxes, and then making sure the remainder was distributed to her trust. Important social goals are met when these functions are performed properly—creditors get their money, the government gets its tax revenue, and the family gets its inheritance.

In the American system, the government makes the first claim on its part of the estate, while the family must be content to wait for what is left. When the Internal Revenue Service has taken its share, it issues a "closing letter," indicating that all tax liabilities have been satisfied. But in the Meding case, the closing letter never came, because John Fairbanks stole the money earmarked for the taxes.[52] Distribution was delayed until after the closing letter, and the delays went on and on. These are the kinds of red flags to which a probate court must respond in carrying out its fundamental duty, to oversee fiduciaries. The long months of delay gave Fairbanks the chance to steal his client's money.

Another vital function of most probate courts is the protection of incompetents or "wards." Fairbanks was named as guardian of Richard Tweedy, a mentally disabled adult. The court's ability to require accounts is the effective check it has on the significant power of a guardian, but the New Hampshire probate court failed year after year to demand Fairbanks' delinquent accounts. When Fairbanks did file his accounts, years late, they were incomplete and suspect. The probate court's inaction undermined one of its most basic functions—to protect the weak and vulnerable from financial exploitation.

Helen Meding was weak and frail when she signed the will naming John Fairbanks her executor.[53] Clients often name lawyers as their executors, not realizing that a family member could serve in the role. There is nothing magic about an executor that requires legal training. A financially savvy layperson may do just as well in managing an estate. He can always hire a lawyer as attorney for the estate to perform any duties that require legal knowledge. If the lawyer does a bad job, the executor can fire her far more easily than removing a lawyer who has been named as executor by the probate court.

The Fairbanks Aftermath

After Fairbanks fled the jurisdiction, his former clients tried desperately to get back their money, money that had been earmarked for retirements, nursing home bills, or grandchildren's educations. They filed claims with the New Hampshire Bar Association Client Indemnity Fund in January 1990, and claims in U.S. Bankruptcy Court. The bankruptcy trustee, Victor Dahar, scheduled a January hearing to question Fairbanks about his assets.[54] But Fairbanks was on the lam and not coming back. Law enforcement could not find him.

Attorney Charles Spanos kept hammering at the attorney general's office for failing to bring an indictment in the matter involving his client Kaarle Lehtinen (from whom Fairbanks had allegedly stolen as much as $250,000). Fairbanks had left Spanos' brother, probate judge Harry Spanos, in serious trouble as well. On January 5, 1990—within a week of Fairbanks' flight—the Supreme Court's Judicial Conduct Committee advised Harry Spanos that it was going to charge him with judicial misconduct.[55] His failure to monitor the probate activities of Fairbanks had come back to haunt him. The court issued an official reprimand to Spanos in September but voted to keep it secret.

By February 1990, the claims of the people Fairbanks had injured totaled more than $3.5 million. Former clients scrambled to attach Fairbanks' property. His homes in Newport and Ogunquit were both held in his wife's name. The New Hampshire Supreme Court disbarred the fugitive Fairbanks in April 1990, while Charles Spanos was being given the runaround by the attorney general's office. First the office said they would pursue the Lehtinen theft, then they reversed themselves. By July 1990, the office had taken the position that Fairbanks did not have the "intention at the time he signed [Kaarle] Lehtinen's name on the check" to defraud Lehtinen, "hence no charges would be brought."[56]

In the meantime, the Supreme Court was reacting to the scandal. On a humid July day, the Supreme Court received a Long Range Planning Task Force report. That report recommended creating a position of judicial administrator for the probate courts, to create accountability and uniformity sorely needed in the New Hampshire probate system. The report went on to recommend that probate court registers be appointed instead of elected and answer to probate court supervision. In the wake of the Fairbanks scandal, the courts and the legal community acted to improve the system, as the New Hampshire Supreme

Court appointed John Maher to the new full-time position of Administrative Judge of the Probate Court.[57]

In March 1991, the federal bankruptcy court ordered John Fairbanks' wife not to sell any property. Twenty-five former clients, two insurance companies, one bank, and the town of Washington, New Hampshire, all clamored for a share of the $6 million Fairbanks was alleged to owe.[58] The case dragged on throughout 1991 until, one bitter November day, the disheartened claimants settled for a few cents on the dollar.[59] John Fairbanks was still nowhere to be found. His family and the New Hampshire bar's client indemnity fund anted up the cash.[60]

The report of the bankruptcy trustee revealed that Fairbanks had stolen money from the trusts and estates of his elderly clients to cover large investment losses. "The investments he made were hardly any different than 20-to-1 on the red six on the roulette table. . . . To me it's ironic he died in Las Vegas," said the lawyer for one Fairbanks victim. He even stole from his own sisters. "Obviously he was leading a double life and we just never realized it," said one sister. "It's like I'm talking about someone else."[61]

Fairbanks' activities affected several generations of his clients' families. Helen Meding's son Stephen said, "It was a terrible thing he did to my family. . . . Financially, it just raised heck with us. We thought this was permanent income. The family was just devastated."[62] The most haunting thought came from Fairbanks' sister on the day his body was discovered: "We lost our brother a long time ago, and it's a great family tragedy."[63]

The Fairbanks story was plucked from the newspapers by *America's Most Wanted, Unsolved Mysteries, Hard Copy,* and *Prime Suspect.* These shows sent the story streaming out to the American public on their television screens.[64] Despite his notoriety, the agile judge eluded capture as one year faded into the next.

Throughout the spring of 1993 and into the summer, the New Hampshire legislature grew more and more frustrated with what appeared to be rather lax efforts to find the celebrated judge. That summer the legislature passed a bill offering a $20,000 reward for anyone who gave information leading to Fairbanks' capture.[65] In October, the bankruptcy court paid trustee Victor Dahar $232,000 in legal fees for his work on the Fairbanks bankruptcy case, a payment that outraged the creditors, who had received a paltry fifteen cents on the dollar.[66]

John Fairbanks was found dead in the Las Vegas hotel room on March 21, 1994. His sordid end, however, did not dampen the firestorm his flight had precipitated. Allegations of judicial misconduct and foot-dragging by law enforcement continued to spawn legislative committees to investigate the debacle.

The Fairbanks' Committees

How could Fairbanks have stolen so much from the trusts and estates he served as executor, trustee, guardian or attorney? Why wasn't he caught sooner, and why did it take so long to indict him? To answer these questions, the New Hampshire Legislature passed a bill in 1996 creating an investigative committee, the Committee to Study the Investigation of the John C. Fairbanks Matter (the First Committee).[67] The First Committee was made up of seven members of the House Judiciary and Family Law Committees. It was charged with considering the "scope and quality of said investigation conducted by any law enforcement agency, the professional conduct committee of the Supreme Court, and the judicial conduct committee of the Supreme Court."[68]

The First Committee met twenty-five times and took testimony from invited witnesses. There was, however, only one hearing for interested members of the public to air their views. Most of those involved in the Fairbanks case testified before the committee, including attorney Charles Spanos.

Spanos addressed the delay in charging Fairbanks that many believed allowed his flight from justice. "Based upon my experience as an attorney for thirty-six years, some of those years representing the state as Sullivan County Attorney and representing defendants in criminal matters, I submit that there was more than sufficient probable cause to charge John Fairbanks with crimes long before December 28, 1989. Had this matter [of Kaarle Lehtinen] been handled more expeditiously, John Fairbanks would not have escaped the punishment that he so rightfully deserved. If these crimes had been committed by some average citizen or some indigent, you can bet that it wouldn't take so long to obtain warrants for their arrest."[69]

Charles Spanos, who had pushed the attorney general's office so hard on behalf of his client, offered several explanations for the delay in pursuing Fairbanks. First, Fairbanks was a reputable member of the community and the state. Second, the attorney general's office was understaffed due to lack of an adequate budget. Third, there was some kind of cover-up. Said Spanos, "I personally do not for a moment believe that there has been any cover-up, but if the public perception exists, then it must be corrected in order to instill in the citizenry confidence in our criminal system."[70]

Spanos' appearance before the First Committee was followed by testimony from members of the Professional Conduct Committee, the group charged with disciplining lawyers in New Hampshire. Chairman Peter Kearns sat before the legislators and tried to defend the process used in the Fairbanks case. He fielded questions as to why the Professional Conduct Committee had failed to prevent John Fairbanks from harming so many clients. Since the Fairbanks scandal, Kearns noted, the committee had added an auditor. It now had the "capability of reacting in a day or less, if information is presented to [the committee], concerning lost, missing, and unretrievable funds."[71]

The First Committee lacked the power to subpoena witnesses, and its efforts were limited. While Fairbanks' civil attorneys sent letters to the committee explaining their activities on behalf of Fairbanks, they did not appear to testify. Fairbanks' criminal attorney, now a federal district court judge, refused to appear unless subpoenaed for fear he would violate the attorney-client privilege. It later became clear that Fairbanks' attorneys knew he had traveled to Quebec City several times before his flight. They did not inform the police even after Fairbanks fled, constrained by their ethical obligations to their client.[72]

The First Committee had more luck with the New Hampshire State Police. On October 30, 1996, the committee heard from Captain Kevin O'Brien, who detailed the efforts of the state police to find Fairbanks, including leads sending them to Florida and the Caribbean. As to the Canadian leads, O'Brien said, "there was no solid information that Fairbanks was in Canada. To be exact, it was the exact opposite. We felt Florida and the southern area, possibly the islands, was the location he had possibly been in."[73]

As it turned out, the police could hardly have been more wrong. Their trip to Tortola, based on a lead from the Fairbanks story on *Unsolved Mysteries* yielded nothing, since, as they learned after his death, John Fairbanks had headed north and not south. State police investigators took a trip to Quebec after the seventy-year-old Fairbanks was found dead. They discovered that their telephone monitoring efforts would never have turned up a lead since "people apparently used pay phones in New Hampshire and a credit card number to call Fairbanks at his residence in Quebec. The calls would be charged to a number in Quebec City and would not show up on toll records of family members' telephone numbers." O'Brien denied that the State Police had ever been asked to "provide any cover for Fairbanks during any stage of the investigation."[74]

The First Committee grilled the Judicial Conduct Committee next. On November 6, 1996, they heard from attorney Frederick K. Upton, chairman of the Judicial Conduct Committee. Upton discussed complaints about disparate sentencing and delays that had been lodged against Fairbanks while he served as a criminal court judge. These had come to the Judicial Conduct Committee through Gov. John Sununu's legal counsel, Stephen Merrill (later state attorney general and governor). Fairbanks was given a private reprimand in 1983 and that ended the matter.[75]

The Judicial Conduct Committee also examined the role of probate judge Harry Spanos in the wake of the 1989 press stories, "relating the apparent widespread looting of decedents' estates and guardianship estates by John Fairbanks as a lawyer and a fiduciary." While the Judicial Conduct Committee recommended a public censure of Judge Spanos, the Supreme Court instead voted to reprimand him privately, in the wake of the Nighswander report about lax enforcement of the probate laws in the Sullivan County Probate Court and the registry of probate. Upton agreed with the First Committee members that New Hampshire had a serious problem of conflicts of interest with part-time probate judges and part-time district court judges simultaneously practicing law.[76]

Chief Justice David Brock represented the New Hampshire Supreme Court in front of the First Committee on November 12, 1996. Addressing the issue of part-time judges, he recommended that New Hampshire (1) establish a full-time judiciary and (2) consider eliminating, by amendment, the unusual constitutional provision that made probate registers elected, constitutional officers. By shaking the New Hampshire legal system, the Fairbanks scandal engendered a new openness in the Judicial and Professional Conduct Committees of the state supreme court. Justice Brock talked about the balance between the accused's rights and the right of the public to open disciplinary hearings. The First Committee also discussed the need for rapid referrals of criminal matters as required by statute. Brock noted that the supreme court was also now "transmitting information about disbarred attorneys to a national database."[77]

But at the same session, former attorney general and governor Stephen Merrill disagreed with the chief justice's proposals, stating that he approved of the part-time system of judges and felt that changing over to a full-time system would not be an improvement. He also opposed the appointment of registers of probate, favoring instead retaining the current method of electing them.[78] So much for reform.

On December 3, 1996, the acting chairman of the First Committee, Rep. Nick Hart, submitted a report for the full committee's approval. The report began by stating that "John C. Fairbanks was permitted to continue criminal activities and then allowed to flee the New Hampshire jurisdiction due to favorable and at times deferential and preferential treatment by the New Hampshire government at many levels, over a period of many years."[79]

The First Committee endured many hours of testimony on the probate system. Their indictment of the Sullivan County probate system was harsh. It was, said the First Committee, "derelict in its duties to enforce state laws concerning reporting procedures relative to accounts and inventories. We find that no initiatives were taken by anyone in that system to alert the Professional Conduct Committee or the Judicial Conduct Committee or the Attorney General's Office about

John C. Fairbanks' failure to comply with New Hampshire law."[80] Had the probate system followed its own rules, it could have spared many victims.

The First Committee leveled strong criticism at the Professional Conduct Committee as well. It found that the Professional Conduct Committee, "conducted an extremely limited and informal investigation into the 1976 Trudeau complaint, the first complaint filed with that committee about John Fairbanks." Even when Fairbanks was removed as guardian of the Coonley-Demers estate in 1987, the Professional Conduct Committee took no action to investigate and did not notify the attorney general's office.[81]

The attorney general's office was painted as, "slow, uncoordinated, and ineffective" in its investigation of Fairbanks. It failed to freeze his assets and only tried to arrest him when it was too late. The report described the office as, "lacking in leadership and communication."[82] After Fairbanks fled, the report charged, the office displayed basic ignorance in investigative techniques.

All in all, the Fairbanks case illustrated, "a systemic failure of government to do its basic duty of protecting citizens from itself." The committee was especially troubled because government agencies time and again dismissed allegations of Fairbanks' misconduct because of his status in the community. The First Committee concluded that Fairbanks was "afforded extraordinary protection from prosecution not provided to ordinary citizens and [they] question[ed] the sincerity of the pursuit of John C. Fairbanks after his flight."[83]

The committee offered a number of remedies for the "culture of trust" that prevailed in Sullivan County and in the the other nine New Hampshire probate courts that operated as "ten different fiefdoms." The laxity in the Sullivan County Probate Court "was conducive to criminal activity through the misuse of clients' funds, but tolerated delinquencies and violations of the law over a long period of time." The remedies the First Committee proposed included (1) clarifying the responsibility of the probate judge for the activities of the register of probate's office; (2) requiring that registers improve the consistency and uniformity of delinquency notices, citations, and contempt charges and that they impose penalties to ensure compliance; (3) requiring adequate staffing and training of probate court employees; (4) reporting lawyer/fiduciaries cited by the probate court for delinquencies to the Professional Conduct Committee; (5) requiring formal training for probate judges in the Canons of Judicial Conduct; (6) requiring that lawyers disclose relationships with banks in which they hold trust accounts; (7) sending notices to beneficiaries when fiduciaries are delinquent in the filing of inventories or trust accounts; (8) conducting mandatory audits of all cited accounts; (9) barring any sale of assets without a power of attorney from the beneficiary or order of the court; (10) entering contempt of court citations immediately if an auditor's request for records is refused; (11) improving the notification of beneficiaries when final accounts are filed by the fiduciary; and (12) recommending that probate and district court judges serve full time.[84]

The First Committee to investigate John Fairbanks felt it had done a thorough job, but it did not propose a specific legislative agenda. The acting chair of the committee observed that "in the past five months we have aired and given vent to a lot of suspicions. New Hampshire is stepping up to the challenge of enforcing the laws already on the books and presenting measures that will prevent this from happening again." Chairman Nick Hart cited evidence of the committee's achievements. The Judicial Conduct Committee and the Professional Conduct Committee had opened their hearings to the public; an administrative judge had been appointed to oversee the ten probate courts and to make those courts more responsive to public need; notification to bonding companies when late filings occurred had been improved; the use of computers in all probate courts to make the filing of accounts routine with automatic notice of late filings to the register of probate had been enhanced; and the Professional Conduct Committee had hired an auditor to investigate lost, missing, or unretrievable funds.[85]

However, even as the First Committee submitted its work to the State Librarian in January 1997, two members felt the need to pursue the matter further. Filing a "minority report," Rep. Richard Kennedy and Rep. Philip Cobbin called for a "more detailed review of Fairbanks' career."[86] Cobbin refused to let the matter die and introduced legislation seeking the creation of a second investigative committee.

The Second Fairbanks Committee

▼

Chairman Alf Jacobson convened a meeting of that Second Committee on October 30, 1997. There were few citizens in the twenty or so seats reserved for the public in the legislative hearing room in Concord. The paneling on the walls and the green carpet of the hearing room paled in comparison to the reds, yellows, and oranges splashed on the trees brushing the windows of the committee room. Jacobson allowed each committee member to offer his or her thoughts on the direction of the committee and its ultimate goals.[87] The committee resonated with the pervasive concern that, as the *Manchester Union Leader* had said, "the shame of Fairbanks has haunted the state's legal community and the courts."[88]

The Second Committee continued to meet through January 1998. The *Union Leader* would later describe its members as "amateurs asked to unravel the mystery of 'a systemic failure of government' in a case of thievery that has haunted New Hampshire for the past nine years and had its roots in a judicial appointment made 40 years ago." The Second Committee met twenty-nine times, talked with forty-nine witnesses, and used its subpoena power to do what the First Committee could not, bring Fairbanks' three lawyers forward to testify. Those lawyers revealed that they knew Fairbanks had traveled to Canada in the months before his flight. However, they were bound by attorney-client privilege not to tell authorities as those authorities were vainly searching the Caribbean for Fairbanks.[89]

Though the Second Committee elicited substantial new testimony, it had no professional investigator assigned and could not determine where the $4–$6 million went. "It would take somebody who would be totally devoted to go through all of the financial records just to see exactly what happened," said Jacobson. Though there was substantial dissension about the language used in the report, the committee recommended (1) that the state require bonding of all fiduciaries to protect beneficiaries of estates from criminal conduct; (2) that the legislature review laws governing "who gets paid" when a court orders distribution of estate funds; and (3) that the state implement standardized accounting and reporting practices for all fiduciaries dealing with the probate court.[90]

Even when the Second Committee finished its work in the winter of 1998, the ghost of John Fairbanks would not die. On October 3, 1999, the *Boston Globe* wrote, "There are still many who believe that the system looked the other way while the state's most corrupt judge slipped away."[91] In March 1999, the president-elect of the New Hampshire Bar Association credited "the never-ending fallout" from the Fairbanks case for continuing legislative efforts to reform that state's judiciary.[92] The great lesson of Fairbanks is that, regardless of procedural safeguards, probate courts that are too cozy are ripe for fraud and abuse. The following chapters offer more evidence of such abuses and further proposals for reform.

Chapter 2

Lawyers as Fiduciaries

Should lawyers be fiduciaries at all? Many people are under the impression that they must appoint a lawyer to be their executor because the job takes some special legal training. This is simply not true. Often, a friend or family member is the best choice for executor or trustee, since that person can supervise the estate's lawyer. The following New York case illustrates some of the monitoring problems that arise when a lawyer for an estate also serves as its sole fiduciary.

Governor Mario Cuomo described him as a "friend and supporter for seven years," and Mayor David Dinkins said, "there was every reason to believe one could place trust in him."[1] They were referring to Arnold Biegen, the man choking back sobs as he stood before New York state judge Daniel FitzGerald on a cold November day in 1992 to be sentenced to a thirty-five-month to nine-year term in state prison for grand larceny.[2] Biegen was admitted to the New York bar in 1959.[3] A successful lawyer and law partner of Philip Klein in the ensuing years, he pled guilty to stealing $886,367 from Klein's elderly, schizophrenic wife, Beatrice. He also admitted stealing $158,000 from the Dinkins campaign fund.[4]

In his will, Philip Klein had named his trusted friend Arnold Biegen to serve as his executor. The surrogate's court respected Klein's wish, and Biegen took over the administration of Klein's estate and the management of Beatrice's finances. Biegen also held a power of attorney that allowed him to write checks on her behalf.[5] Beatrice Klein lived alone on Parade Avenue in Flatbush, in a home with a view of

Prospect Park. Philip and her late sister Mimi left her in excess of $850,000, more than enough money to care for a frail widow living in a small New York apartment.[6]

Biegen hired social worker Holly Gemme in 1990, asking her to visit Beatrice and take care of her many needs. Over the next several years, Biegen wrote checks for all of Beatrice's expenses, including Gemme's fees, nursing care, and rent.[7] Gemme regularly visited Beatrice Klein and tried to ease her suffering from schizophrenia.[8]

The fifty-seven-year old Biegen was busy at his white-shoe, Manhattan law firm, Parker, Chapin, Flattau & Klimpl.[9] He became a fundraiser for the mayoral campaign of David Dinkins, and by 1991 he had ascended to the office of treasurer of the Dinkins reelection committee. Gov. Mario Cuomo next tapped Biegen to serve on the powerful Judicial Screening Panel.[10] His place in the New York political world seemed secure.

But in early 1992, prosecutors in Manhattan District Attorney Robert Morganthau's office began probing rumors that Biegen had stolen as much as $158,000 from the Dinkins campaign. State investigators began looking at Biegen's accounts at Bank Leumi, a review that lead them to Biegen's thefts from the Klein estate.[11] The investigators discovered that Biegen had written 142 checks to himself from Klein's Bank Leumi account between August 1989 and February 1991. The "former confidant" of Mayor Dinkins and Governor Cuomo later "confessed that he took Klein's money for his 'personal use.'"[12]

The New York Surrogate's Court, an institution notorious for its corruption and cronyism, had little or no role in uncovering Biegen's looting of the Klein estate. Although Biegen was subject to the court's oversight as the named executor of Philip Klein's estate and the estate of Beatrice Klein's sister, Mimi Cohn, his breach of fiduciary duty was only uncovered by the Manhattan D.A.'s office as the accidental by-product of a political corruption probe.

Biegen had actually resigned as Dinkins' campaign treasurer in January 1991, in the wake of an internal audit that disclosed the missing $158,000.[13] The Manhattan D.A.'s office secured indictments against Biegen on January 31 and February 7. Biegen decided on a secret guilty plea to both campaign theft and the looting of the estates on February 10, 1992.

The New York press got hold of the story and would not let go. At a City Hall news conference they demanded to know from Mayor Dinkins why his campaign had failed to report the thefts to law enforcement once Biegen admitted them. Dinkins responded that "his campaign was under no obligation to report the thefts to the police or to prosecutors because it had disclosed them in its campaign finance disclosure statements, signed by Mr. Biegen himself." The campaign's lawyer, later Clinton White House operative, Harold Ickes, said, "he and other top campaign officials . . . made a decision not to press charges against Mr. Biegen because they had hoped to receive repayment from him."[14]

As of February 1992, however, only $7,000 remained in Beatrice Klein's account at Bank Leumi, and she was "living in squalor."[15] Holly Gemme, the social worker hired by Biegen, had not been paid for nearly three months and was becoming increasingly suspicious of her employer. She began to see press accounts of Biegen's "withdrawals" from the Dinkins campaign fund and put two and two together. Filing an action in Kings County Supreme Court, Gemme asked the court to appoint a conservator for Beatrice Klein to protect her from the very man her husband had trusted to care for her.[16]

On February 7, 1992, Judge Sebastian Leone appointed lawyer Jerome Becker to investigate the Klein estate.[17] Becker, an attorney at the New York law firm of Davidoff & Melito, was appointed Beatrice Klein's conservator. Becker joined Manhattan attorney Margaret Bomba, the court-appointed receiver of Klein's estate, to examine Biegen's bank records, Klein's accounts, and the estate accounts. The two lawyers considered strategies to make their client and ward whole. On February 19, 1992, Becker told the press that "we're going to look at some of the relationships with the law firm to see whether or not Biegen was properly supervised as a partner."[18]

The beleaguered New York Lawyers Fund for Client Protection, the state reimbursement fund for the victims of attorney fraud, required that a lawyer's firm be sued first before it would reimburse a victim for losses. Executive Director Frederick Miller stated, "While we stand ready to help in an emergency situation . . . we think ultimately the responsibility is Biegen's. And next in line is his law firm." In the years before Biegen's theft was discovered, the fund had been rendered virtually insolvent by a run of cases, and it had reduced its per victim payout from $100,000 to $50,000.[19]

A New York case, *Clients' Security Fund v. Grandeau,*[20] had established the principle that "partnership law dictate[s] that, ordinarily, one member of a partnership is liable for the tortious conduct of another, and any member of a partnership may be liable for a conversion of property committed by a member of the firm, even where the other members of the firm had no knowledge of the offending partner's action."[21] The lesson for clients was to go to a law firm with more than one attorney. The Lawyers' Fund had "never reimbursed a client loss involving a partnership of three of more attorneys, despite the millions of dollars it has paid to clients of solo practitioners."[22]

The day the court appointed Jerome Becker to serve as Beatrice Klein's conservator, Arnold Biegen resigned from the state's Judicial Screening Panel, citing "unfortunate events." Cuomo had kept Biegen on the panel after his term expired in April 1990 since, as Cuomo's spokesman put it, "there was no sense of urgency to replace Biegen . . . because the panel had been inactive."[23]

Biegen's woes continued as he pled guilty on February 10, 1992 to charges of grand larceny. In entering his pleas, Biegen alluded to information he could provide to Morganthau's office implicating Mayor Dinkins, Sen. Alphonse D'Amato, and others in political corruption. The federal and state authorities were interested, but, in their opinion, Biegen never came through.[24] In May 1992, Biegen pled guilty in U.S. District Court to two counts of tax evasion for failing to pay income taxes on the money he stole from Klein and the Dinkins campaign.[25]

In an effort to forestall his disbarment, Biegen tried to resign from the New York State Bar.[26] The bar rejected this attempted end-run, and on April 7, 1992, more than thirty-two years after he was admitted to practice, the First Appellate Division confirmed Biegen's disbarment on the basis of his felony convictions. The name Arnold Irwin Biegen was stricken from the roll of attorneys under New York Judiciary Law s90(4)(a), which provides that, "Any person being an attorney and counselor-at-law who shall be convicted of a felony . . . shall upon such conviction cease to be an attorney and counselor-at-law or to be competent to practice law as such."[27]

Biegen's downfall sparked press reports of vigorous efforts to uncover political corruption both in the Dinkins campaign and elsewhere, but the only result of the ensuing probe was the Parker Chapin law firm's admission they made $22,000 in illegal campaign contributions. The firm paid a $150,000 fine.[28] Biegen did not get off so lightly. On October 29, 1992, he was sentenced in federal court to thirty-five months in prison.[29] Then, in November, state court judge Daniel Fitzgerald meted out a thirty-five month to nine-year term in state prison, to run concurrently with Biegen's federal sentence.[30]

In May 1992, *Newsday* reporters following the Biegen case reported that "[Biegen] confessed he took Klein's money for his 'personal use.'" He had written 142 checks to himself from Klein's account. Many were for clothes for family members and for other personal expenses.[31] He paid $18,000 to decide a legal matter with another law firm and $15,000 to a Long Island landscaping company for work on his East Hampton beach house.[32] He led an expensive lifestyle befitting a successful Manhattan lawyer; it just happened to be one he could not afford.[33]

In the end, Biegen served his time in a federal prison, and *Newsday* reported in October 1992 that Beatrice Klein "was reimbursed for the stolen funds."[34] Parker Chapin paid its fine, and the sordid matter ended with no further bombshells about politicians dipping into the till. Arnold Biegen had betrayed Philip Klein's trust, and therein lies a useful lesson for all testators: Think twice before naming a lawyer as executor. There may be better candidates for the job, and a lawyer may have a conflict of interest in seeking the position in the first place.

Should Lawyers Be Fiduciaries

Helen Meding and Philip Klein chose lawyers, John Fairbanks and Arnold Biegen, as executors of their estates. Perhaps they thought an executor needed special legal knowledge and ability. Perhaps they knew no one else to take the position. Whatever the reasons, Meding and Klein did not have to choose a lawyer to perform this role. A layperson could have done the job. In fact, there is an ongoing debate about whether lawyers should act as executors or trustees at all.

The term *fiduciary,* "is derived from the Roman law, and means a person . . . having [a] duty, created by his undertaking, to act primarily for another's benefit in matters connected with such undertaking."[35] The fiduciary must act with "scrupulous good faith and candor."[36] These qualities were conspicuously lacking in Fairbanks' dealings with his incompetent ward Richard Tweedy and in Biegen's treatment of his elderly client Beatrice Klein. These lawyers' breaches of fiduciary duty raise the question of whether they were appropriate choices for the job of executor. But the broader question of whether lawyers have inherent conflicts created by their appointments as executors, trustees, guardians, or conservators also merits discussion.

As anyone who has seen *The Paper Chase* knows, law professors train their pupils to "think like lawyers." That film portrayed a Hollywood version of the grueling first year of law school, where professors are handed students with "heads full of mush" to transform into sharp, analytical thinkers who can spot a legal issue a mile away. Somewhere in the process, law students absorb the doctrinal substance that makes up contracts, torts, civil procedure, criminal law, and the other courses of the traditional law school curriculum.

Because lawyers are steeped in legal rules and their analytic abilities are honed in law school, they seem well suited to the duties involved in representing the elderly, the disabled, and the dead.[37] A clear understanding of the law lends itself to fulfilling the duties imposed by statutes and case law on executors and trustees. The ethical training provided by law schools and the regulation of the legal profession (though both could use improvement) should, arguably, produce good candidates for fiduciary positions.

What then are the downsides of making an attorney a fiduciary? They may not be obvious to most clients. If a lawyer drafts the instrument that names her as executor, it may raise issues later, when the lawyer is paid a fee for her work as executor. If the client is frail, there is the specter that the lawyer may have exercised undue influence by pushing the client to name her as fiduciary. If a lawyer represents a client during the client's life and then becomes the executor post-death, new duties arise to the client's children, grandchildren, and any other heirs or beneficiaries. This kind of "multiple representation" can generate conflicts of interest—real or imagined—in the lawyer/executor.

The ethical rules in the legal profession have frowned on lawyers asking clients to name them as executor. Historically, the profession's position was that "so long as the client originally had the idea for the attorney to serve as fiduciary, then there were no ethical violations."[38] The publication in 1969 of the Model Code of Professional Responsibility (the Model Code), a set of ethical aspirations and prohibitions, set the stage for a more precise explication of the concern about solicitation in this realm. Ethical Consideration 5–6 provided that, "[a] lawyer should not consciously influence a client to name him as executor, trustee or lawyer in such instrument. In those cases where a client wishes to name his lawyer as such, care should be taken by the lawyer to avoid even the appearance of impropriety."[39] But ethical considerations were not prohibitions, they were merely goals to which lawyers should aspire.[40]

The 1983 ABA Model Rules of Professional Conduct (the Model Rules) that replaced the Model Code, dropped Ethical Consideration 5–6. The Model Rules subsumed the issue under the more general conflict-of-interest rules 1.7 and 1.8. An original draft of the Model Rules said in the commentary that a lawyer should not seek to have himself named in an instrument as executor, but the comment was dropped from the final edition.[41] The 1983 Model Rules took a step backward by not protecting clients from lawyers who might prey upon them by insinuating themselves into their wills.

The American College of Trust and Estate Counsel (ACTEC) is an organization of lawyers expert in wills, trusts, and estate planning. ACTEC has, over the years, tried to bridge the gap between the Model Rules, which are written with litigators in mind, and the world of trusts and estates lawyers. Its position is that, "An individual is generally free to select and appoint whomever he or she wishes to a fiduciary office (e.g., trustee, executor . . .)." Thus, ACTEC stated, "As a general proposition lawyers should be permitted to assist adequately informed clients who wish to appoint their lawyers as fiduciaries. Accordingly, a lawyer should be free to prepare a document that appoints the lawyer to a fiduciary office so long as the client is properly informed, the appointment does not violate the conflict of interest rules of [Model Rule] 1.7, and the appointment is not the product of undue influence or improper solicitation by the lawyer."[42]

Unfortunately, in a recent recommendation adopted by the American Bar Association House of Delegates, a commission charged with reforming the Model Rules (known as "Ethics 2000") proposed language that may lead lawyers to believe it is acceptable to solicit a client's nomination as an executor or trustee. The Ethics 2000 recommendation provided that the Model Rules do not prohibit a lawyer from seeking (which is synonymous with "soliciting") to be named executor of the client's estate or to another potentially lucrative fiduciary position.[43] A better approach would have been to provide that a lawyer is not prohibited from accepting an appointment as an executor or trustee. Perhaps the American Bar Association will revisit this issue or individual states will alter the language when they consider adopting the new Ethics 2000 recommendations. The remaining language in the Ethics 2000 recommendation improves on the Model Rules, as it emphasizes that the lawyer should disclose to the client any conflicts of interest in this kind of situation. This disclosure essentially requires informed consent and a waiver of the disclosed conflict by the client before the attorney proceeds to name himself as executor or trustee in the instrument.

Lawyers may be the best choice as executor or trustee for some clients. Elderly clients may have long relationships with and great confidence in their lawyers. Given the mobility of families in twenty-first-century America, those clients may have tenuous connections to their children or siblings who may live in other parts of the country. And if a court is looking for a guardian for an incompetent adult, lawyers well-versed in fiduciary responsibilities, who are constrained by ethical rules and malpractice concerns, are prime candidates for the job. However, the financial interest that such lawyer/fiduciaries have in acting as executor or trustee may affect their judgment and create a conflict of interest. As long as the client understands this, there should be no problem. But with elderly and infirm clients, there is always the issue of whether any consent to such conflicts is truly "informed."

ACTEC defines an informed client in part as one who is "provided with information regarding the role and duties of the fiduciary, the ability of the lay person to serve as fiduciary with legal and other professional assistance, and the comparative cost of appointing the lawyer or other person or institution as fiduciary."[44] A client must understand that in addition to an executor, his estate will need an attorney. Counsel for the estate must have legal expertise. When a lawyer is named as executor, he or she faces the task of hiring a lawyer for the estate, and therein lies one of the ethical pitfalls of this situation. Can a lawyer/executor really make a detached judgment in choosing counsel for the estate. Will he simply hire himself for that second role?

Clients should understand this duality of roles and the potential conflicts between them. Clients often wrongly assume that the executor must perform the legal tasks involved in probate of the estate or managing the trust. They do not realize that a lay person/executor can hire a lawyer to perform these tasks. However, there is no bright line between an informed client who initiates a discussion about the wisdom of naming his lawyer executor and an uninformed client whose lawyer solicits the job. Probing the murky waters of the decision making process after the client is dead is difficult or impossible.

In states that allow "double dipping"—payment for work as executor plus payment for work as lawyer for the estate—lawyers act as executors in about 10 percent of the cases probated. In states that frown on double dipping, only 1 percent or 2 percent of the estates have attorney/executors.[45] These statistics suggest that money is a primary motivation in the decision to take on the role of fiduciary in addition to that of fiduciary's lawyer. This monetary incentive, and the often close relationship between elderly client and savvy lawyer, creates a potential for abuse. Removing the lawyer's incentive to do both jobs should reduce the temptation to solicit the nomination as executor; the statistics indicate that it does. This may be a better way to curb abuse by attorneys than an outright ban on lawyers as fiduciaries, which some commentators have proposed. In many cases a lawyer is the appropriate choice as executor, trustee, guardian, or conservator, and the number of institutional trustees, like banks, is dwindling. Well-trained lawyer/fiduciaries may fill this gap for clients.

Commentators in this area have worked to establish a model that would allow lawyers to act as fiduciaries when it makes sense, for instance, when there is no one else available and the client's assets do not warrant the expense of a corporate fiduciary. In their *Fordham Law Review* article, Edward Spurgeon and Mary Jane Ciccarello examine the benefits and the costs of having a lawyer serve as a fiduciary.[46] They argue that lawyers should continue to act as executors, trustees, or guardians but lawyers acting in these roles should receive more guidance. They cite the American Bar Association's effort to provide ethical guidance in the Section on Real Property, Probate and Trust Law's "Principles for Attorneys Acting in Other Fiduciary Roles."[47] This set of nine principles is aimed at ensuring that attorneys chosen as fiduciaries protect their clients' interests. Principle 9, "Role of the Attorney in Advising the Client," emphasizes that "[r]egardless of whether the attorney is named as a fiduciary, it is the responsibility of the attorney to advise the client as to the considerations affecting the choice of an appropriate fiduciary."[48] Greater disclosure should expose the overreaching attorney bent on becoming an executor, but, as the Biegen case demonstrates, such safeguards do not always work.

In many of the most egregious cases in this book, the lawyers involved were not simply lawyers for the executors or trustees but were themselves the fiduciaries. As a result, many of my proposals focus on lawyer/fiduciaries. How can a court ensure that the appointment of an attorney as executor is appropriate, and what is needed to increase the probate court's scrutiny of such cases? Some lawyers express no concern about attorney/fiduciaries, arguing that in an era of tough competition, the number of Americans needing fiduciaries is increasing, and taking on the role of fiduciary is a way to expand one's practice.[49] But many more in the legal profession and in the academy realize that if lawyers are to continue to act as fiduciaries, there must be increased protection for those who rely on their trustworthiness.

Many commentators acknowledge that the scent of undue influence hangs heavy over drafting attorneys who name themselves as fiduciaries in their clients' wills or trusts. Jeffrey Pennell of the Emory University Law School cites an attorney that he greatly admires, Floyd McGown, for the rule of thumb that a smart lawyer should not, "accept service as a fiduciary in a trust or will created by a client."[50] While there may be exceptions, "the practical reality is that being named as a fiduciary or as an attorney for a fiduciary [in the will itself] raises eyebrows; the presumption is that impropriety resulted in the designation unless the attorney can establish otherwise."[51]

New York attorney Joshua Rubenstein echoes this sentiment: "Attorneys who have represented individuals and families over a period of many years are frequently uniquely qualified to serve as executors for such individuals. Indeed, it is the norm rather than the exception in England and in certain parts of the United States, in particular the Boston area, for attorneys to serve as executors. In New York, however, the phrase 'attorney/executor' or 'attorney/fiduciary' might be uttered in the same breath as 'carpetbagger' with the result that the nomination of an attorney as an executor is regarded by many as presumptively bad. The fact of the matter is that in no other area of the law is the abuse, and the potential for abuse, so great as in the area of attorney/executors, who have temporary legal title to assets that belong beneficially to someone else."[52]

The profession could allay public distrust of lawyer/fiduciaries by (1) amending the applicable ethical rules; (2) pursuing legislative changes regarding attorneys fees in such cases; and (3) advocating legislative changes to the procedural rules of estate administration. The next few chapters explore some of these proposed reforms.

Chapter 3

Probate Avoidance

▼

The American probate process has long been perceived as slow, expensive, and corrupt. Some have capitalized on this perception by encouraging Americans to avoid probate by using nonprobate devices like living trusts. While such devices can be used to streamline the transfer of property at death, their lack of probate court oversight can lead to abuse. The next case illustrates the downside of probate avoidance.

In 1964, James Gunderson moved his young law practice into the sales office of Leisure World, a palm-trimmed retirement community in Orange County's Laguna Hills, south of Los Angeles. It was an enterprising move for an attorney who would, over the years, counsel as many as seven thousand Leisure World residents on the mysteries of probate and estate planning.[1] Leisure World was home to a burgeoning population of elderly and financially comfortable retirees—men and women who had flocked to post–World War II southern California from all over America to shape a life in its brilliant sunshine and tropical breezes.

Merrill Miller was one of those retirees. His father, John Miller, had been a practicing lawyer and a medical doctor in Montana. There, he successfully defended a man on trial for murder, and the grateful client promised that he would be forever in his debt. The client subsequently joined the Chicago banking world, while John Miller moved to Illinois to practice medicine.[2]

There, Miller met an enterprising fellow physician with a small but promising business in his apartment. His friend desperately needed capital to grow his tiny business, so he asked Miller if he could lend him $100,000. Miller's medical practice did not afford him such a pool of disposable income, but he told his friend that he had a former client turned banker who might be able to help. Miller introduced the entrepreneur to his former client and the deal came together. Miller's friend was Dr. Wallace Abbott, and the business was Abbott Laboratories.[3]

Remembering Miller's past favors, Abbott gave him the West Coast distributorship of Abbott Laboratories. The company subsequently bought it back from him in exchange for stock. At his death, Miller left the stock to his children, who, in turn, left most of their shares to their last surviving sibling, Merrill Miller.[4]

Merrill Miller retired to Leisure World, where he lived a frugal and unassuming life, apparently unaware of the magnitude of his fortune. He once told a friend that he had always wanted to buy a fruit orchard but could never afford it.[5] Miller met James Gunderson in 1972. He was seventy-eight when he and Gunderson began a "social relationship, taking frequent trips with mutual friends, celebrating birthdays and holidays and enjoying weekly luncheons."[6] James Gunderson was like that, the kind of old-fashioned lawyer who took the term *counselor* to heart, mixing business with pleasure and spending social time with his elderly clients, much to their delight.

In 1973, Gunderson handled Merrill Miller's sister's estate, and in 1974, he drafted a will for Miller himself. Later that year, Miller amended his will with a codicil. The will named Gunderson and Miller friend Walter Perry as the coexecutors of the estate, to share the duties and responsibilities of probate when Miller passed on.[7]

Over the next ten years, Miller consulted periodically with Gunderson about his estate plan. They made several changes to the plan until 1984, when Gunderson advised Miller to execute what is referred to colloquially as a "living trust."[8] Legally known as "inter vivos, revocable trusts," these instruments are an effective vehicle for avoiding the probate process post-death.

The "grantor" of a living trust executes the trust with a mere signature, and thereby transfers all of his or her assets—stocks, bonds, house, cars—into the trust, and retains the power to change or amend the trust at any time. Typical provisions state that the trust assets shall be distributed to the "beneficiaries" (usually children, grandchildren, or favorite charities) upon the grantor's death. These trusts are created before death and have an immediate legal existence (thus the appellation "living" trusts). Through the vagaries of probate law, they avoid the probate process altogether.

While revocable, inter vivos trusts do indeed avoid probate and may minimize its immediate costs. They can, however, create administrative costs of their own that may be greater than the probate savings. Lawyers must be paid to draft the trusts and trustees to administer them. While the grantor is alive, he or she is often the only trustee. So it was with Merrill Miller's trust. He was the first trustee. James Gunderson, in the very instrument that he drafted, was named Miller's successor. According to plan, Gunderson took over as trustee in 1988, and Miller gave up control of his trust assets, giving Gunderson complete power over $17 million.[9]

In August 1988, Gunderson prepared an amendment to Miller's trust that gave him more shares of Abbot Laboratories stock as a trust beneficiary. By 1990, Gunderson, presumably concerned about the appearance of impropriety in drafting instruments that made him a beneficiary, brought in "independent counsel" Ellsworth DeWeese, his former partner.[10] Much later, in legal proceedings filed against Gunderson, it came out that DeWeese had copied verbatim provisions drafted by Gunderson. DeWeese also sent Gunderson a letter saying "Call me if I done wrong," hardly the words of an independent attorney for Miller![11] DeWeese also sent to his own file a memo asserting that Miller had asked for a certain will provision giving Gunderson power over his property. It was shown later that DeWeese had not discussed the trust amendment with Miller.[12]

In January 1992, James Gunderson contacted DeWeese about a final amendment to Miller's trust. DeWeese prepared the trust amendment, and "[o]n January 14, DeWeese and Gunderson drove to Miller's home to execute the new trust and will provisions. Gunderson waited until Miller signed the documents. Gunderson signed the originals and gave them to DeWeese for copying."[13]

The original 1984 trust, drafted by Gunderson, included a gift of $300,000 worth of Abbott Labs stock to Gunderson. That gift was increased in a 1988 amendment to the trust. Finally, in the January 1992 amendment to Miller's will and trust, the gift was increased to a one-fifth share of all Abbott Labs stock, to be paid to Gunderson and his children on Miller's death.[14] What was not obvious was that Gunderson's one-fifth was exempt from estate taxes, thus yielding him 41 percent of the net estate after tax.[15]

Death came to Merrill Miller soon after the amendments were signed, and within the month, James Gunderson transferred five thousand shares of stock to the Gunderson children's trust. Five thousand more shares followed soon after. James Gunderson's daughter Linda, also an attorney, was the trustee of the children's trust.[16]

Gunderson drafted away, ignoring the long-standing California case *Magee v. State Bar,* that had struck down a $20,000 gift included to an attorney in a will the same attorney drafted. *Magee* suggests that "attorneys should avoid drawing wills containing gifts to themselves under circumstances in which there is a reasonable suspicion that the client was overreached or that the gift would prevent the attorney from acting in the client's best interests."[17]

The profession claims to frown on lawyers drafting gifts to themselves, and Model Rule 1.8(c) provides that a lawyer ". . . shall not solicit any substantial gift from a client . . . or prepare on behalf of a client an instrument giving the lawyer or a person related to the lawyer any substantial gift. . . ."[18] But the California Rule of Professional Conduct (CRPC) governing this matter is far less specific. CRPC 4-400 merely prohibits a lawyer from "inducing a client to make a substantial gift, including a testamentary gift," to the lawyer or his or her family unless lawyer and client are related.[19] Commentary on the rule suggests that if the gift is fair and appropriate, the lawyer may draft an instrument that includes the gift.[20] Only if the gift is a result of undue influence is discipline by the state bar appropriate.

CRPC 4-400 left a hole wide enough to drive a truck through and James Gunderson drove away with the goods. When challenged, Gunderson's position was that he did not induce Merrill Miller to make the $3.5 million gift of Abbot stock; rather, Miller was so grateful for

Gunderson's assistance and friendship over the years that he insisted on making the gift.[21] It turned out Gunderson was blessed with other such grateful clients. He managed to secure "title to one square mile of land in San Bernardino County" and a 316-acre farm in Fresno County from two other clients.[22]

In another case, "Gunderson inherited nearly $250,000 in AT&T stock from a Canadian woman who had been declared senile five months before Gunderson prepared her last will and testament, making himself the estate's major beneficiary."[23] In the case of Mary Hall, Gunderson drafted a will that failed to mention a power Hall held to determine the ultimate recipients of the trust proceeds. The trust gave Gunderson the power to distribute trust assets if Hall did not exercise the power. Gunderson used this power to distribute the remainder of the estate to himself after Hall's death. Gunderson testified that the woman wanted him to inherit all her belongings.[24] All these facts came to light at the civil trial commenced by Merrill Miller's heirs and beneficiaries when they discovered that the attorney who drafted the majority of Miller's instruments was to share up to 40 percent of Miller's estate.

The Trial

▼

Harry Westover is an expert in estate matters and a member of the prestigious American College of Trust & Estates Counsel (ACTEC). Merrill Miller's heirs approached Westover when they began to see the shape of Miller's estate plan. Westover contacted his cousin John Westover and John's son William, experienced trial attorneys in Phoenix, Arizona, to discuss taking the case. The beneficiaries, Mary McWethy, Dr. George Plain, Doris McWethy Plain, Richard McWethy, and Capt. Robert McWethy, were relatives who shared three-fifths of Miller's remaining estate equally. William Kellogg and Walter and Barbara Perry were friends who split the last one-fifth of the estate. The Westovers knew they were taking on a difficult case. There was a clause in the document (a so-called no-contest clause) that provided that the beneficiaries would forfeit their bequests if they challenged the instrument. The clause simply compounded the usual difficulty lawyers face in discerning evidence of wrongdoing in the murky waters of conflict of interest and undue influence.

Miller's heirs began their quest for justice with a petition—a query to the probate court on October 9, 1992, asking whether a lawsuit against Gunderson would trigger the no-contest clause that he had inserted in the trust. Two months later, in December 1992, the court opined that it would not trigger the no-contest clause and that the parties could safely proceed without putting their bequests at risk. The beneficiaries then filed a second petition seeking a declaration that Miller's gift to Gunderson and his children was void. The Westovers' legal strategy was to force Gunderson to hold the stock he was bequeathed in a "constructive trust," a court-ordered remedy to recapture assets that have been procured by fraud or other unjust means.

Not only did the court give the beneficiaries the green-light to sue, but on his own motion, probate court judge Tully Seymour also stripped James Gunderson of his role as trustee, citing a lack of public confidence as his motivation. "There is a tremendous amount of distrust, suspicion and fear in the legal community and the Leisure World community."[25]

Gunderson responded to these concerns six days later by distributing "virtually all of the Abbott Laboratories stock [in the Gunderson children's trust] . . . to the five beneficiaries," Gunderson's own five children. On December 22, beneficiary Mary McWethy asked the court to force Gunderson to account for the stock as well as a $25,000 legal fee paid to his daughter Linda for preparing federal tax returns that she did not in fact prepare.

In preparing for an all-out attack on what they perceived to be a serious ethical and moral failure on Gunderson's part, the Westovers benefited from reporters who gave them information as they uncovered it. The press also unearthed an asset—an original Charles Russell painting—transferred for less than market value to the husband of Gunderson's secretary and later sold for a tidy profit. Like Deep Throat who aided journalists Bob Woodward and Carl Bernstein in the book *All the President's Men*, a "mystery lady" regularly phoned in information to the attorneys that helped uncover the painting. Other cases, like Mary Hall's estate, were uncovered by dogged determination and detective work. On the eve of trial in the spring of 1994, the Westovers had built a strong case showing a pattern of misconduct by Gunderson that they hoped would help their clients force him to disgorge the $3.5 million in stock he had received from the bedridden and blind Merrill Miller.

After months of waiting and preliminary court rulings that forced Gunderson to turn over extensive information from his files, the trial began. Armed with a mountain of evidence, John Westover finally got the chance to grill James Gunderson on May 19, 1994. Westover knew that to convince the judge (jury trials are not available in probate matters in California) that the $3.5 million bequest was not made voluntarily by Miller, he would have to link it to a long series of similar bequests by Gunderson clients. Westover had to show a pattern of misconduct. The question was would Judge Byron McMillan admit testimony of such "prior bad acts" in evidence? John Westover knew he had won a critical strategic victory when Judge McMillan agreed that the other cases uncovered by the plaintiffs were indeed relevant to the Miller case and admitted evidence of Gunderson's conduct in relation to other clients' wills and trusts.

When Westover got him on the witness stand, he "quizzed Gunderson about another inheritance of $250,000 received from a Leisure World woman who had been declared senile about four months before Gunderson prepared her last will and testament, making himself the estate's major beneficiary. The [woman's] heirs sued, and Gunderson reached a confidential, out-of-court settlement with them that included a payment by Gunderson of $60,000."[26]

Gunderson's defense was that Miller, like many of Gunderson's other elderly and infirm clients, wanted him to have the $3.5 million as a token of their friendship. Gunderson declared in his testimony that Miller was healthy and alert in 1990. During the course of discovery and at trial, Miller's friends testified that they had to read to Miller and "heard his complaints about not being able to see." They stated that Miller did not recognize them when they entered a room. Ellsworth DeWeese claimed that Miller recognized him when he came into the room, although longtime friends like Harold Stromsen and Jane Perry said otherwise. Gunderson admitted that Miller would ask who had walked through the doorway, but he denied this indicated that Miller was blind.

> By January 1992, he could not see well enough to distinguish his [not legally] adopted granddaughter from his caregiver. He could not see well enough to use a 52″ T.V. He did not know what day or time of day it was. And he could not hear sufficiently to identify who was speaking. His housekeeper, Nancy Lopez said his conversation was confused. He even forgot his name. . . . Mr. Gunderson acknowledged that Mr. Miller should not have a checkbook and that he had tried to take it away from him. Yet Mr. Gunderson, thereafter, with his good friend, Ellsworth DeWeese, caused Mr. Miller to execute a new will, one containing a dispository provision never discussed with Mr. Miller and about which a record was fabricated.[27]

On January 7, 1992, Merrill Miller executed a new trust amendment, leaving his lawyer and his lawyer's children's trust $3.5 million. On January 26, 1992, his doctor found him "virtually dead," responding "only in monosyllables."[28] Merrill Miller died February 27, 1992, at the age of ninety-eight. At trial, the evidence established that Miller had told his friends that he had always wanted a fruit orchard but Gunderson told him he did not have enough money to buy one. At various times, Miller told friends that he was leaving Gunderson 5 percent or 1 percent of his estate.[29] The January 1992 amendment resulted in Gunderson's children's trust receiving 41 percent of Miller's net estate.

Brick by brick, John Westover carefully built a wall of evidence that was impossible for Gunderson's counsel to get around. By June 17 when the testimony ended, the veteran trial lawyer had proved his case. In response to Gunderson's defense that Miller had wished him to inherit 20 percent of his stock in Abbott Laboratories, Westover said, "This man did the most despicable [thing] he used his position of trust not for those who relied upon him, but for himself. . . . James D. Gunderson was not a friend of Merrill A. Miller's. James D. Gunderson was an exploiter."[30] In the end, Judge Byron McMillan agreed.

After hearing testimony from expert witness, Dr. John Boyer, head of the Center on Aging at the University of Arizona College of Medicine that "there would be little question that (Miller) was demented in the last two years"[31] and from Gunderson's former partner Ellsworth DeWeese, who drafted the last Miller trust amendment, Judge McMillan found that:

> (1) Gunderson acted as Miller's attorney from 1974 until his death, thereby creating a fiduciary obligation to Miller; (2) Gunderson commenced preparing testamentary instruments for Miller in 1974; (3) Gunderson prepared and participated in the execution of the 1984 inter vivos trust in which Gunderson was named a beneficiary and Miller the trustee, activating a presumption of fraud and undue influence; (4) Gunderson prepared and participated in the execution of several amendments to the inter vivos trust from 1984 through 1988, each carrying the presumption of fraud and undue influence; (5) Miller resigned as trustee in 1988 and Gunderson assumed control of all the trust assets as successor trustee, thereby creating a fiduciary relationship with Miller; (6) Gunderson prepared amendments to the trust from 1988 to February 1990, each of which gave rise to the presumption of fraud and undue influence; (7) Gunderson made arrangements for DeWeese to act as attorney to Miller in preparing an amendment to the 1984 trust and complete restatement of the trust, but was not independent counsel, thereby raising a presumption of fraud and undue influence; (8) Gunderson continued to prepare and participate in the execution of amendments to the trust and the presumption continued; (9) Gunderson contacted DeWeese in 1992, gave directions to DeWeese about the preparation of new testamentary instruments for Miller, actively participated in the preparation and execution of such instruments, thereby continuing the presumption of fraud and undue influence; (10) Gunderson breached his fiduciary duty to Miller by preparing testamentary instruments naming himself as beneficiary and misleading Miller as to the contents of such instruments; (11) Gunderson breached his fiduciary duty to respondents by delivering to himself and his attorney-partner and daughter, Linda Gunderson, and subsequently selling 20 percent of the Abbott Laboratories stock held by the trust; and (12) Linda Gunderson had actual and constructive notice of respondents' claim to the Abbott Laboratories stock she received and her subsequent sale of the stock constituted a breach of her fiduciary duty owed to respondents.[32]

Judge McMillan imposed a constructive trust on the ten thousand Abbot Labs shares already transferred. In a second action for an accounting, the probate court entered judgment against James Gunderson for breach of fiduciary duty. Gunderson appealed, and the California Fourth District Court of Appeal upheld the general findings of the trial court as to undue influence and breach of fiduciary duty, concluding that, "Pursuant to the terms of the trust he created, Gunderson received stock worth several million dollars. Not only did he obtain benefits for himself, but members of his family received substantial gifts as well. The gift of Abbott Laboratories stock, which also benefitted Gunderson's children, and full control of Miller's possessions, strikes us as an undue benefit to the drafting attorney."[33]

Probate Avoidance

▼

James Gunderson made a practice of drafting living trusts for clients who named him as trustee or successor trustee.[34] In the Miller case, he took over as successor trustee.[35] Gunderson's abuse of these revocable trusts led the California legislature to enact a provision discouraging drafting attorneys from serving as sole trustees of such trusts.

Orange County's chief probate judge, Tully Seymour, expressed the growing concern with these nonprobate vehicles in a letter to the *Los Angeles Times* dated December 20, 1992. A reader had asked how Gunderson had "[persuaded] Superior Court probate judges to approve such wills for probate?" Seymour responded, "It should be noted that inter vivos or 'living trusts' are private documents that are not filed with the Probate Court. Under a living trust, the trustee distributes the estate without any court supervision. The only way in which the court can acquire jurisdiction over a living trust is if one of the beneficiaries or other interested parties files a petition with the court questioning the conduct of the trustee." Seymour acknowledged a need to review California's probate rules and ethical rules to prevent future scandals.[36]

The push for living trusts initially came through a book written by

Norman F. Dacey and published in 1965. Aptly titled, *How to Avoid Probate*, it sold millions of copies. Dacey captured the public impression of probate when he wrote, "the probate system, conceived generations ago as a device for protecting heirs, has now become their greatest enemy. Almost universally corrupt, it is essentially a form of private taxation levied by the legal profession upon the rest of the population. All across the land, both large and small estates are being plundered by lawyers specializing in 'probate practice.'"[37] Dacey included a simple form "Declaration of Trust" in his book that did manage to avoid probate.

Was Dacey right? That depends. Probate costs vary widely from state to state. They range from $3,150 on a $100,000 estate in California to $5,000 for the same size estate in New York. A $600,000 estate might generate $13,150 in fees in California and up to $22,000 in New York.[38] Most states still base the executor's fees on a "statutory fee schedule," a percentage of the value of the probate estate, regardless of actual work. As for the attorney's fees—a separate charge—some states authorize the same percentage of the estate's value as is provided for the executor, but many are turning to a "reasonable fee" for the actual time spent and work done. In states that pay attorneys by the percentage method, "extraordinary" fees may be added for work such as preparing tax returns. Either way, dying does cost money.

However, paying for probate does generate benefits. Creditors are foreclosed from bringing actions against the heirs for the decedent's debts, the court supervises the executor and requires accountings that should reveal any wrongdoing, and the court provides a neutral forum for relatives who have disputes about the decedent's property. In the cases handled by attorneys Fairbanks, Biegen, and Gunderson, the court failed to provide these benefits, however. At least in theory, this is what a citizen pays for through probate fees and charges.

The probate process can last from twelve months to several years; the average is about eighteen months. Lawyers and nonlawyers alike stress probate delays and costs when selling clients a living trust. The California attorney general's office has pursued several so-called living trust mills, nonlawyers (sometimes with a lawyer involved) who sell living trust kits to senior citizens for thousands of dollars. The California State Bar has pursued these people for the unauthorized practice of law as well.

Before there were living trusts, the average American avoided probate either by holding property in joint tenancy with right of survivorship or through buying life insurance payable to spouses or children. With the rise of the pension trust in the last several decades, qualified retirement plans have become another pervasive nonprobate asset. Some people avoid probate by simply failing to file anything with the court at the time of a family death. This failure can come back to haunt them when they later want to sell Grandma and Grandpa's house. There will likely be a problem with clear title. One of the primary functions of probate is to maintain clear title to real estate and other valuable assets. But why does the law allow some property to pass to heirs and takers without going through probate? If probate has such an important function and is such a money-maker for lawyers and the government, why allow avoidance devices like living trusts at all?

This is the puzzle that John Langbein, a preeminent scholar of probate and succession, addressed in his seminal *Harvard Law Review* article, "The Nonprobate Revolution and the Future of the Law of Succession." After discussing the growth of nonprobate assets and transfers in late-twentieth-century America, including trillions of dollars in life insurance and billions more in pension plans, joint property, and revocable trusts, Langbein said, "The puzzle in the story of the nonprobate revolution is not that transferors should have sought to avoid probate, but rather that other persons whose interests probate was meant to serve—above all, creditors—should have allowed the protections of the probate system to slip away from them." Langbein credits "a series of changes in the nature of wealth and in the business practices of creditors" for pushing probate into a subsidiary role in American succession law.[39]

It was the prominence of real estate and the need to maintain clear title that shaped probate law in the nineteenth century. Langbein writes that the title-clearing function of probate is now far less important because the average American owns less land and more contractual assets. These kinds of assets, like life insurance and pension plans, have built-in administrative mechanisms to enforce the written beneficiary designations of decedents and pay the beneficiaries at death. Only when there is a dispute among contractual beneficiaries or ambiguity about who is the beneficiary do the courts become involved in the distribution of nonprobate assets.[40] So too with revocable trusts. The trustees of such trusts have the power to distribute property out of the "living trust" without court permission.[41]

The second change Langbein identifies is reduced creditor reliance on the probate system to collect debts. Langbein interviewed many credit officers who noted that most survivors pay the decedent's debts voluntarily, especially consumer debts. The majority of these debts are nominal, and the survivors feel either a moral or a legal obligation to clear them up. Probate is a last resort for these creditors, and they tend to utilize it only if the debts are over a certain amount. Otherwise, a cost-benefit analysis shows the action is not worth it.[42]

Most states now offer their citizens semiformal ways to distribute assets without resort to a full-blown or "formal" probate process. These include short-form proceedings for small estates (usually from $20,000 to $100,000) that reduce the paperwork and court time required to pass the decedent's property on to the recipients. Similar devices exist for passing specific assets, like cars, through the use of a simple affidavit. These statutory devices have minimized the need for formal probate in many cases.[43]

The question remains why American law allows probate and nonprobate transfers, which look extraordinarily similar, to be subject to different rules and different systems. Langbein describes the disconnect as a legal fiction, prompted by courts who "sympathize with people who want to avoid probate."[44]

The public's fear and loathing of probate has been a driving force in the National Conference of Commissioners on Uniform State Laws efforts to reform the probate process through the model Uniform Probate Code (UPC). In the states that adopted the 1982 UPC amendments, citizens have available a much simpler form of transfer that echoes the civil law's "universal succession." "In European law, survivors settle decedents' estates without court involvement unless there is a contest or special difficulty."[45]

The UPC creates a similar type of succession—voluntary succession without court intervention so long as all the beneficiaries are in agreement and there are no disputes—that takes the court out of probate. Langbein cites scholars like Richard Wellman, the principal draftsman of the UPC, who have agreed that "The assumption that administration of an estate requires a judicial proceeding is as doubtful as it is costly." Langbein concludes, "As long as probate reform still calls for probate, it will not go far enough for the tastes of many transferors, who view probate as little more than a tax imposed for the benefit of court functionaries and lawyers."[46]

A look at Merrill Miller's case reveals both the legitimate and illegitimate uses of the nonprobate device called a living trust. While Miller's $17 million estate was not tied up in probate or subject to statutory executor's and attorney's fees, the trustee, James Gunderson, was able to transfer stock from the living trust within days of Miller's death.[47] Although the stock was ultimately disgorged by the Gunderson children's trust, this took the expertise of a specialized litigator and many months of effort. Gunderson also took fees for acting as trustee. He also paid $25,000 to his daughter, Linda Gunderson, for preparing tax returns that were eventually prepared by someone else.[48] If Merrill Miller could look back from the next world, he might have seen that the siren song of "living trusts" includes the sour note of lack of judicial oversight and potential for abuse.

If Merrill Miller's living trust had been a will, the probate court would have seen that Gunderson was a major beneficiary, and it might have cried foul. Unfortunately, this kind of attention to the terms of a will may be an illusion in probate courts as large as those in Orange County. Later reviews of court files showed Gunderson as drafting attorney, counsel to the estate, and beneficiary in several cases, which should have sent up a huge red flag for undue influence. The probate court processed those wills with few if any questions.[49]

Judge Tully Seymour warned the public of these gaps in the probate system when he wrote to the *Los Angeles Times* in response to its investigative article. Seymour said, "With approximately 5,000 attorneys in Orange County, it is often not apparent that a person named in a will is an attorney. The present probate system relies on notice being given to all of the heirs that a will is being probated. If an heir has an objection, the heir can file a will contest challenging all or part of the provisions of the will."[50]

Seymour acknowledged that "the recent problems that have been revealed indicate inadequacies in the existing system."[51] He correctly characterized the burden on the probate courts. But one is left to wonder if the problem is not simply judicial overload but also the inbred atmosphere of courts like that in Sullivan County, New Hampshire, and the failure of the legal profession's ethical rules to circumscribe more specifically practices such as attorneys' naming themselves as fiduciaries in instruments they draft.

The Aftermath

The Gunderson case became public on November 22, 1992. A *Los Angeles Times* reporter published an account detailing several of the cases that John Westover would eventually use in his presentation to the probate court. The reporter, Davan Maharaj, interviewed James Gunderson in August 1992. Gunderson declined to discuss the details of the Merrill Miller case, "that recently made him $3.5 million richer, or other, similarly questionable cases that turned up in a *Times* investigation that included interviewing more than 100 people and reviewing more than 100 court cases handled by the attorney." Gunderson cited attorney-client privilege for his silence.[52]

The *Times* piece set off a firestorm. Within days, the Orange County Sheriff's Department had launched its own investigation.[53] For the first time in its history, the Orange County Bar Association also initiated an investigation, and its then-president said that "his organization would be willing to investigate any complaint filed against Gunderson by the lawyer's clients or heirs of former clients."[54]

Two days after the story appeared, the chief probate judge in Orange County, Tully Seymour, announced his own investigation and review of all cases in which James Gunderson or his law partners had been the attorney, trustee, or conservator.[55]

On November 25, the State Bar jumped on the Gunderson bandwagon. "In a departure from the organization's policy of refusing comment on such matters, State Bar President Harvey I. Saferstein said that probate lawyer James D. Gunderson . . . is being investigated for receiving substantial bequests from his clients under questionable circumstances, for allegedly taking actions that were not in the best interest of his clients and for potential conflicts of interest." Saferstein characterized the decision to confirm the investigation as, "an emergency measure meant to protect the public" and confided that the state bar had received "many" calls from citizens who had read the *Times* piece and demanded to know if the bar were going to sanction Gunderson.[56]

By December 1992, the public guardian's office was looking into the Gunderson matter, and Judge Tully Seymour, on his own motion, removed Gunderson as trustee of the Miller trust and as guardian of another Leisure World resident, ninety-two-year old Gladys Grove. On December 12, Seymour took action when the public guardian's office, the office supervising court-appointed guardians, could find only $230,000 of the reported $1 million in Grove trust assets that Gunderson had been allowed by the probate court to control.[57]

John Westover, in an effort to comply with the ethical requirement that lawyers report the misconduct of other lawyers, sent a letter to the state bar reporting the facts of the Miller case. He asked that the bar stay any action until the civil litigation was over. He did not want to be accused of filing a disciplinary complaint to gain strategic advantage in a lawsuit. The state bar never acknowledged Westover's letter, but belatedly demanded information from the Westovers about the Gunderson case.[58] Concerned that the public's perception of California lawyers was being tarnished, Harvey Saferstein, along with Chief Trial Counsel Robert Heflin, met with the *Times* staff in December. "I have asked my board committee on rules to look at the ABA's model rule and to look at [our rule] to see if we can change it," Saferstein said at the meeting. He acknowledged that the ABA rule and the rules of thirty-eight other states explicitly prohibited an attorney from drafting a will or trust that gave the attorney a substantial gift.[59]

Saferstein discussed the prospect of enhancing probate court review of all wills and trusts to watch out for inappropriate gifts to attorneys, but he acknowledged that doing so might place an unrealistic burden on the already overburdened probate courts.[60] He later indicated that a change to CPRC 4-400 to conform it to the ABA model rule was in the offing, but the change never materialized. In 2003, despite the lessons of Gunderson, CPRC 4-400 remains unchanged. In the meantime, the ABA's Ethics 2000 Commission continues to tighten up Rule 1.8(c).[61]

During 1993, California politicians picked up on the public "distrust, suspicion and fear" engendered by the Gunderson scandal. In February 1993, Orange County lawmakers won committee approval for a bill to prevent lawyers from establishing themselves as beneficiaries of their clients' estates."[62] The bill, AB 21, was passed by both houses in July 1993, signed by Gov. Pete Wilson, and took effect on January 1, 1994.[63] The law invalidates gifts to drafting attorneys absent a "certificate of independent review." It also addresses the problem of drafting attorneys who name themselves sole trustees of living trusts. Such nominations would be presumed invalid by the courts, absent independent certification that they were made with informed consent of the client. Clearly, the legislation was aimed directly at Gunderson.[64]

Just as the legislation his conduct had spawned took effect, James Gunderson resigned from the practice of law. In January 1994, one step ahead of a state bar bringing conflict of interest charges against him, Gunderson handed in his ticket, citing health issues.[65] He retired to his home in San Juan Capistrano. His name would forever be linked with the scandal that prompted this change in California probate law.[66]

The Gunderson case may have raised red flags if it had been within the purview of the probate court. Unlike Fairbanks and Biegen, Gunderson named himself as an actual beneficiary of the trust instrument. One hopes that such an obvious example of overreaching would have been noticed by a probate court and investigated. Gunderson's actions did prompt the California legislature to regulate the legal profession, and the resulting legislation was heavily criticized by some members of the bar as unnecessary or poorly drafted. One lesson from Gunderson may be that if the bar fails to think hard about reform, state legislatures will.

Chapter 4

Complexity and Corruption

Was Norman Dacey correct when he asserted that the probate system is a corrupt and unnecessarily complex government bureaucracy? And if he was, is avoiding probate the answer? We have seen that both the probate and nonprobate systems of transferring wealth in this country are vulnerable to abuse. Perhaps an effort to blend the two systems is the correct approach to reform. But before discussing the modern efforts to do just that, let us examine why traditional probate is so complex and whether it must be so.

Mayor Fiorello H. LaGuardia called New York's probate court (known there as "surrogate's court") "the most expensive undertaking in the world." As one report from 1977 noted, "Often, the patronage can be blatant. In one extreme case 11 years ago, Joseph A. Cox, who was retiring as Surrogate, said he had named as special guardian to a large estate the son of his fellow Manhattan Surrogate, S. Samuel DiFalco. The assignment was a 'wedding present' for the younger DiFalco, Mr. Cox said."[1]

Arcane probate procedures seem byzantine to the average American. In part, the complexity reflects the multiple purposes of probate. Probate has three functions: (1) making property marketable (title-clearing); (2) paying off the decedent's debts (creditor protection); and (3) implementing the decedent's donative intent regarding the property remaining once creditors claims have been discharged (distribution).[2] Each purpose requires a number of separate actions by the decedent's personal representative. Those actions are dictated by state legislatures and state courts.

The complex rules of probate procedure are found in each state's statutes, in a compilation typically called the "probate code." Within this code are statutes on a broad array of topics: the execution of wills, intestacy (a set of rules determining which family members inherit if there is no will), and rules on notice to be given when someone dies. Each county or court may have its own "court rules" that are an overlay on the state statutes. In addition, each state has judicially created case law that interprets the statutes.

The first step in the probate process is to petition the court to appoint an executor or administrator (the "personal representative"). The personal representative must inventory and transfer the decedent's assets to a "common pot." There are rules governing the transfer of a decedent's real property, securities, bank accounts, and other assets. Banks, brokerage houses, and county registrars of deeds must be contacted to have the title to these assets transferred. The personal representative must present to the institution proof as to the rightful owner of the property. Someone must arrange for a new title to be prepared. This is a time-consuming process and, while it is not legally complicated, it is essential to creating clear title for the property's new owners.

Next, the estate is required to provide creditors with notice of their debtor's death. The personal representative must publish notices in the newspaper and send specific notices to known creditors of the decedent. Again, this requires time and effort. The court requires proof that notice to creditors has been given, which may require appearing in court.

Paying taxes is another important step in the probate process, and the rules of the estate tax, like all tax rules, are remarkably complex. Laypeople, and many lawyers, are unable to complete a federal estate tax return. They must hire an accountant. The federal estate tax form, Form 706, is complicated, and may require the preparer to secure a number of documents, including forms from insurance companies and, most time-consuming, a costly set of asset appraisals for real property, jewelry, artwork, and any stock in closely held corporations.

Experts for each asset must be contacted, given the necessary information, and paid for their expertise.

When the money remaining in an estate is to be distributed, the probate system has rules to determine who is entitled to it. The personal representative must be acquainted with the rules that determine who is an heir and what happens if a beneficiary is dead. The personal representative often must search for heirs. This too may require the assistance of an expert and costs money. When the heirs or beneficiaries are paid, the personal representative must get receipts and releases.

Finally, the personal representative must file an accounting, detailing the assets she received at the beginning of the process, all the money spent for creditors, tax authorities, and, finally, heirs and beneficiaries. This accounting is a time-consuming process, but it is necessary for the fiduciary to be released from liability at the end of the probate process. Each of these activities is more difficult if the heirs or beneficiaries are minors and cannot consent to financial decisions. If minors or unborn beneficiaries may benefit from a trust or estate, a guardian ad litem (a court-appointed attorney to review the accounts and consent on behalf of the minor) may be required. The personal representative of an estate must be familiar with the rules governing the form of the account and the peculiarities of local court procedure.

Adding to the complexity, there are generally two parallel sets of rules for inheritance law. This is a consequence of the American tradition of freedom of testation. Allowing Americans to give their property away through the device called a will necessitates a set of rules for "testacy," dying with a will. But the law must also provide a "default" system. This is "intestacy," a set of rules that govern distribution when someone dies without a will. Since more than 70 percent of Americans die without wills, this default system is frequently used.

While a testator may name an executor in his will, those who die without wills express no preference as to who should be the administrators of their estates. Many states have statutes prescribing an order of appointment (for example, spouse, then child, then sibling). But when those people are not able to serve, the court may choose someone in the probate system, like a lawyer in the community, to act. In the same way, when a minor is the beneficiary of an estate or trust, the court may need an objective voice for the child in consenting to fiduciary actions. Again, lawyers are well suited for the job. Assets also need valuation, and some states, like California, require that appraisals be conducted by court-appointed "appraisers" or "referees." These appointive positions present opportunities for favoritism and nepotism.

The more complex a government bureaucracy becomes, the more easily it may become corrupted. This is especially true when large pots of money are involved, as is the case in guardianship, trust, and estate matters. Large amounts of cash, sometimes sitting untapped for months or years, are a tempting target for the occasional unethical court-appointed fiduciary. Unlike sophisticated clients who can monitor their attorneys, elderly, minor, or deceased clients are hardly in a position to do so. The complexity of the probate process and the vulnerability of those served combine to create a climate ripe for abuse.

Stories like that told by Norman Dacey in his book, *How to Avoid Probate,* illustrate the problem with probate court appointees. Dacey recounted the story of Walter E. Hermann who,

> died in Reno, Nevada, leaving a $3 million estate. His son, named as executor, hired the lawyer who drew the will to attend to its probating. To "guard" the interests of the "absent heirs"—three adult daughters who'd been bequeathed $20,000 each—the executor's attorney asked the court to appoint an attorney who practiced in a city 500 miles away. That's equal to the distance from Boston, Massachusetts, to Richmond, Virginia—he was more "absent" than were the absent heirs! (The executor's attorney later explained his nomination by saying that he owed the distant attorney a favor.) But the distant lawyer didn't want to be traveling those 500 miles, so he persuaded the probate judge to appoint a third lawyer, who practiced in the city where the will was being probated to represent him.[3]

Dacey was also highly critical of the practice of court-appointed appraisers. As he wrote, "When you die, the probate court will appoint two or three complete strangers to appraise your estate. The executor whom you have appointed in your will, helpless before the legal mumbo jumbo with which the probate process has been surrounded, will hire a lawyer to do the job. . . . The two or three court-appointed appraisers will then be called in and invited to sign their names at the bottom of the page. Each will then be handed a check representing a chunk of your estate. They did no work of any kind to earn the fee paid to them. . . . The system of appraisals is the single area of probate where there has been any significant reform in recent years, but the disgraceful system has not been wiped out: 30 percent of the states still allow it."[4]

Some studies indicate that fewer than "half the adult deaths in this country are followed by formal administration."[5] The state statutes and court rules that apply to the probate process do not generally apply to nonprobate transfers. The appeal of Dacey's book, with its instructions for opting out of probate, is clear. However, the probate rules are the product of a legitimate effort to protect creditors and heirs. And while the nonprobate process may avoid the complexity of probate, it does not always escape the corruption. As the Gunderson case in Chap. 3 demonstrates, substantial abuses can come from the lack of court oversight over inter vivos trusts. The irony of Norman Dacey's lifelong obsession with helping citizens avoid probate is that it has lead many senior citizens to embrace a vehicle that strips the process of passing assets at death of any oversight and invites abuse by unscrupulous lawyers and family members alike.

The American Model of Probate and Probate Reform ▼

The National Conference of Commissioners on Uniform State Laws (NCCUSL) is a national group comprised of lawyers, judges, and academics, whose members are appointed to represent each of the fifty states. In the 1960s, partly in response to the wave of antiprobate sentiment embodied in Norman Dacey's book, NCCUSL launched a project designed to produce a streamlined, uniform set of probate statutes that states could adopt to modernize and improve their probate procedures. In 1969, this effort, lead by prominent academics like Richard Wellman of the University of Georgia School of Law and Lawrence Waggoner of the University of Michigan Law School, culminated in the publication of the Uniform Probate Code (UPC).[6] The code has been adopted in its entirety by more than fifteen states, and parts of the UPC have been incorporated into the law of virtually every state.[7] The UPC's publication signaled the willingness of at least one segment of the profession to push for improved probate procedures and to help reduce the pain and expense probate involves.

The underlying philosophy of the UPC was that the state should act in probate matters only when called upon by the parties.[8] While it does provide an alternative for a supervised process, the UPC assumes that most estates will not require a supervised process.[9] The drafters have moved away from court intervention to the realm of unsupervised probate. The theory of unsupervised probate is that "unless there is a compelling reason, once an executor or trustee is appointed, the court should step back and let the fiduciary administer the estate and close it without court intervention."[10] Academics, some judges, and many lawyers have moved toward this position in large part because of public complaints that probate involves excessive delay and cost.[11] The movement toward unsupervised probate also reflects the growing importance of nonprobate assets and the desire to pull the probate process closer to the model for the transfer of nonprobate assets like joint property, living trusts, and life insurance.

This academic and legislative response to the real and perceived problems of probate is laudable, as it attempts to bring real world solutions to real people. While unsupervised probate responds to public concerns about expense and delay, for some people, and in some special circumstances, there well may be a need for increased supervision of the probate process. For example, the court should be given the discretion to inquire more closely and to order supervised administration where a lawyer both drafted the instrument in question and is named in it as executor or trustee. And there is an argument for mandatory supervised probate when the court appoints a lawyer unknown to the decedent.

Under the UPC, a court may approve a petition for supervised administration in three different circumstances: (1) if the will directs it, unless circumstances have changed and it is no longer necessary; (2) if the will directs unsupervised administration, but the court concludes that there is a real need to protect the beneficiaries; or (3) if the will is silent and "the Court finds that supervised administration is necessary under the circumstances."[12] In order to protect the public from the potential abuse of a drafting attorney/fiduciary, the UPC drafters should consider building in the option for courts to unilaterally order supervised administration if a lawyer/draftsman has failed to provide his client with disclosure of all the potential conflicts this role entails.

Evidence of disclosure by the lawyer and informed consent from the client might include a certification from an independent attorney at the time of execution; signed disclosure statements outlining fees, alternate choices for fiduciary, and the nature of supervised administration; or a videotape of the client stating that he understands these issues and is voluntarily appointing the lawyer. Appropriate exceptions could be built into the statutory language in the case of a lawyer who is related to the testator, for example, a daughter/lawyer administering her mother's estate.

Admittedly, informed consent and disclosure documents can be the product of undue influence as easily as the will itself can. However, mandatory supervised administration in every such case is overbroad because many decedents do make an informed choice to name their attorneys as executors.

When a court appoints a lawyer previously unknown to the decedent as a personal representative, there is a much stronger argument for supervised administration, particularly if there are no close relatives and the only potential beneficiaries are distant kin living out of state. The lawyer in such a case has had no dealings with the decedent, and the decedent has shown no preference for the lawyer.

Supervised administration under the UPC does not mean that the personal representative must check with the court prior to every action. It does mean that the personal representative's letters of appointment must be endorsed, to indicate to third parties, like banks or brokerage houses, that the personal representative needs permission from the court to take actions like buying or selling securities.[13] The UPC's drafters should consider amending the code to impose such restrictions on a drafting attorney/fiduciary where disclosure has not been made nor consent obtained, or when the court is appointing a lawyer/fiduciary in an intestacy. These restrictions would help prevent the misappropriation of liquid assets in bank accounts or brokerage accounts. Other restrictions may be appropriate as well.

In addition, the UPC drafters might also consider amendments making it impossible to waive the lawyer/fiduciary's bond or accounts without disclosure. The UPC now provides that a court may require bond unless the will waives the requirement.[14] Waiver of bond in a will should be subject to the same disclosure and informed consent requirements as the nomination of a drafting attorney as a fiduciary. The lawyer/fiduciary should have to establish that the testator understood the risk of waiving bond. For court-appointed lawyer/fiduciaries, bond should be mandatory.

Waiver of accounts by naive beneficiaries is another recurring problem in instances of lawyer/fiduciary abuse. The UPC drafters could provide that a drafting lawyer/fiduciary closing an estate must file an accounting.[15] Although making accountings mandatory makes administration more costly, such costs must be weighed against the benefits of preventing of lawyer/fiduciary abuse.

The costs to the probate system of the amendments recommended above are minimal. The changes will not affect the vast majority of estates, for which drafting lawyers do not serve as fiduciaries. These changes will impose a marginally greater cost on the small percentage of cases that do involve drafting lawyer/fiduciaries, but those costs are worth the benefit of increased court oversight over lawyers who maintain enormous power over the assets of decedents. This proposal thus minimizes the costs to the overall system by targeting a narrow group of cases that the legal profession can regulate and has an interest in overseeing—probate matters where drafting lawyers accept appointments as fiduciaries or where the court appoints lawyers who are strangers to the decedent.

While supervised administration will help minimize abuse in certain kinds of probate cases, it does not address the problem of living trusts, which pass outside the probate court's jurisdiction. Article VII of the Uniform Probate Code tried to harmonize the treatment of these trusts with the system of probate wealth transfer, and to streamline the procedures for administering them and providing a forum for disputes.[16] NCCUSL recently approved the new Uniform Trust Code (UTC), which essentially replaces Article VII. The UTC drafters should consider similar authority on the part of the court to intervene when a trustee is also the attorney who drafted the trust. They could model these changes on the California statute that provides a mechanism for scrutinizing and removing a drafting attorney who is also the sole trustee of a trust, a provision implemented in the wake of the Gunderson case.[17] The new UTC might prevent abuse by including similar scrutiny and provisions for removal of such sole trustees, in the absence of proof that they made full disclosure to the client and that the client gave informed consent.

When it comes to a court-appointed trustee of the trust who does not know the grantor/beneficiary at all, the UTC should provide for increased supervision of the trustee. Given the abuse of living trusts by lawyers detailed in the previous chapters, more court oversight over drafting attorney/trustees or court-appointed trustees for elderly clients might minimize the damage to trust beneficiaries. Again, this would only affect a small number of cases, and the additional cost may be worth the added protection. Additional protections could be afforded by adding language to the UTC provisions regarding the duty to account and the obligation to post bond. The drafters might make annual accounts and bond mandatory whenever the sole trustee is also the drafting attorney, which would prevent naive beneficiaries from waiving either requirement.

These proposed changes are based on the premise that it is unusual for a testator or grantor to use a drafting lawyer as fiduciary, though some feel that given the shrinking supply of banks willing to offer such services, lawyers should be trained to fill the gap. While I agree, I think that the challenge to the drafters of the UPC and the UTC is to preserve the overall noninterventionist structure of the codes, which works well for most trusts and estates, while at the same time providing increased scrutiny when "red flags" arise. Such red flags include drafting attorneys petitioning to act as executors or assuming the role of sole trustee of a living trust. If the codes' drafters (and the states that adopt code provisions) can incorporate limited changes that increase court scrutiny in these few cases, while preserving the codes' overall "bystander" approach to most cases, the public will be better served.

Chapter 5

Delays and Deception

▼

The cases described so far illustrate how long it takes to detect fiduciary deception. How can the probate court better identify negligence and theft by executors, trustees, or guardians? The ethical and procedural reforms discussed in Chapters 2 and 4—requiring disclosure by drafting attorney/fiduciaries and increasing the authority of the probate court to ask questions about such appointments at the beginning of the process—would help. The inherent conflicts of interest and the risk that family members may be left uninformed warrant such unilateral inquiry by the probate court in cases involving drafting lawyer/fiduciaries. Closer scrutiny of such cases might detect potential malfeasance during the nominating process and thus spare the beneficiaries the damage that might later be done.

Probate courts have always had the tools to detect malfeasance, if they chose to use them and if the testators or beneficiaries do not give up these protections "voluntarily." For example, the waiver of accounts by naive testators and beneficiaries often exacerbated the damage done in the cases described in previous chapters. The account is an important tool for the probate court in monitoring fiduciaries. Account filing is the linchpin of probate protection. It is the cornerstone of the oversight process, and failure to file accounts should alert the court to potential deception. John Fairbanks in Chapter 1 was a prime example of a fiduciary whose failure to file accounts foreshadowed greater malfeasance.

The final account is supposed to list the assets the fiduciary received at the start of the probate process. This list gives the probate court a starting point to trace the path of those assets as they are invested, used to pay bills or taxes, or distributed to the beneficiaries. The account should then list every additional asset and item of revenue received by the estate during the probate period. For example, wages paid after death, income from rental property, or dividends on stocks should be entered into the ledger. Set against these assets are the estate's liabilities, as in any good balance sheet.

The fiduciary should list all expenditures out of the estate, including funeral home bills, the final hospital bill, mortgage payments on real estate, credit card debts, and any taxes due. If distributions to beneficiaries have been made prior to the final account, they too should be listed. The personal representative must then list the final balance on hand. Trust accountings and guardianship accounts will vary since they are done on an ongoing basis. However, their purpose is the same—to give the court and the beneficiaries a detailed record of the fiduciary's dealings with the assets entrusted to him or her.

Once the final account has been compiled, it is presented to the probate court for approval, along with a proposed order of distribution. The court is supposed to review the account and give the beneficiaries a chance to object to items that are ambiguous or missing. If the beneficiaries do not object, the court typically approves the account and releases the fiduciary from any further liability. The court also approves the personal representative's fee at this point.

If the beneficiaries do object to the account, the court schedules a hearing to air their grievances. If the court finds improper handling of estate funds, it can require the fiduciary to make up any amounts not properly paid out, or the court can remove the fiduciary if it appears there has been a breach of duty. These tools are effective weapons in the fight against fraud and abuse, but they must be used in a timely fashion to reveal unethical or illegal behavior by an executor, administrator, trustee or guardian.

Most states provide that the beneficiaries may waive their right to object to an account, and in some cases to waive the accounting altogether. This makes sense if ethical lawyers are involved and there is no acrimony among the beneficiaries. However, waivers may also be used to cover up the misdeeds of a fiduciary bent on misappropriating assets.

In addition to delays in filing accountings, some lawyers have reported cases of "creative accounting" where fiduciaries create bogus creditors and pay them out of estate assets. The accounting looks normal, and this kind of fraud is hard to discover or to prevent. Other problems include the lack of uniformity from county to county, which may make it hard for judges and other lawyers to see problems in an account. But despite all of these issues, the most chronic failure of the system is the continual judicial forgiveness of late accountings. The failure to file accounts should trigger an immediate response on the part of the probate court. State legislatures should fully fund probate court budgets to provide computerization and enough court personnel to stay on top of delinquent accounts.

The Impact of Technology on Detection

Computers can be extremely useful in allowing probate courts to track cases and to flag those that have dragged on too long. The dusty files of the Sullivan County Probate Court described in Chapter 1 demonstrate the need for a modern tracking system for court files. In many courthouses, litigants and lawyers still go up to a counter and request an overburdened clerk to find a file folder full of paper documents. The file may be on a different floor with the judge's staff, or it may be lost in transit. The papers in the file may have been misfiled, or if the file has been pored over by other lawyers or litigants, the papers may be out of place or missing. This system of recordkeeping is untenable in the age of computers.

If probate files were scanned into computer databases, judges, clerks, and probate staff could access the records without transferring and potentially losing or misplacing files. Simultaneous access ensures more efficient delivery of information during court hearings or during the processing of documents filed with the clerk's office. Computerization also minimizes the risk of lost or misfiled documents within a probate file.

The downside of technology is primarily the cost of training and then paying personnel to load the documents. There are related costs for the acquisition of hardware and software. Some efforts to computerize court records have been a debacle, such as the effort to computerize child support records in California. After millions of dollars were invested in a computer system, the state scrapped the effort because the system never worked properly.[1] In New Jersey, an effort to put real property and land title records in computerized form was such a disaster that the professionals who search title sued the county for interfering with their livelihood. Title records pulled by examiners indicated that the Virgin Mary owned many parcels of land in the county, a surprising result that revealed a glitch in inputting the name of a church with land holdings.[2]

If adequately funded, however, the computerization of probate court records could minimize the problems of lost files and delay. Heirs and beneficiaries could access information more readily, information that could signal lawyer/fiduciary malfeasance. In addition, the Internet promises to deliver even more efficiency and opportunity to detect fiduciary misconduct. Computerized files and records would, of course, cost states and counties enormous sums. The federal estate tax, which will continue to generate revenue during its ten-year phase-out period, might be offered to the states to help finance a broad program to computerize state probate court records.

Los Angeles County has launched a pilot program that uses the Internet to allow probate attorneys to view "probate notes" from their offices. The probate court staff typically goes through the paperwork filed by the attorneys and makes notes of things that need to be clarified or documents that need to be added to the file. Probate attorneys previously had to go to the courthouse to check these notes, return to their offices, and gather the missing information or make the needed corrections. They would then go back to the court to complete the file. Time is money, and the cost of this time-consuming process was passed on to the estates in the form of fees.

The pilot program allows attorneys to view the probate files through the Internet and to see what they need to change or add to a particular file. This kind of innovation dramatically reduces the expenditure of attorney time and thus the cost of the probate process. If such programs were extended to allow attorneys, fiduciaries, heirs, and beneficiaries to view probate files (which are public documents) via the Internet, they would provide increased opportunity to monitor the behavior of fiduciaries. Heirs or beneficiaries could see the probate notes that indicate missing information or late accounts, which could be an early warning of trouble with the fiduciary. They could also view accounts more quickly and have their own accountants examine the documents for discrepancies or missing information.

The court itself could randomly audit fiduciary accounts more cost effectively if they were computerized. Bar authorities could implement mandatory random audits much more inexpensively. As things now stand, an auditor must go physically to the lawyer's office to examine paper records. If privacy were an issue, or if the court found a compelling reason to seal records, the court could restrict access by issuing a password to only those parties with a valid reason to view the records.

Random Audits

There are other actors in the legal system who can work with probate courts to enhance detection. The disciplinary agency and bar association in each state can help. They can use tools like random audits and share the information they gather with probate courts to protect citizens. Random audits are already used by various bars to check client security or "trust" accounts, the accounts in which lawyers hold client funds. These accounts may contain money from a real estate settlement, payments from an insurance company for a personal injury case, or a variety of other funds that belong not to the lawyer but to the client. The idea behind random audits is that lawyers who might be dipping into client funds are most effectively detected by a "surprise" audit of their books.

After a scandal in Virginia, the bar there recommended random audits of fiduciary accounts. The committee that examined the issue expressed "ignorance"as to which of the existing Virginia rules governing client security accounts applied to fiduciary accounts held by a lawyer as an executor, trustee, or guardian. "Even the Vice Chair of the General Assembly's Joint Courts of Justice Ad Hoc Subcommittee Studying Legal Ethics, Client Fraud and Embezzlement—himself an experienced trusts and estates practitioner, expressed surprise when Bar Counsel testified last September that Canon 9 applies to accounts maintained for a traditional trust or estate, and not just a law firm's escrow account."[3] The Virginia lawyers' ignorance of these rules is not unique. While state bars across the country have integrated ethics into continuing legal education programs, this issue seems to need clarification.

Those states that do apply the general rules for client security funds to trust and estate accounts should make an effort to let their bar members know about it. Those that do not should extend those rules to cover fiduciary accounts explicitly. As the Virginia committee concluded, "a properly administered program of random reviews will promote self-education by lawyers and their firms, and a higher level of care and greater uniformity in the handling of client funds. In addition, such a program can reduce temptation and, in some cases, result in earlier detection of dishonesty of both lawyers and members of their office staff."[4]

According to a recent American Bar Association (ABA) survey, eleven states have a program of random audits.[5] In *State of Florida v. Lauren Ann Sill,* the theft of client funds was finally detected through a random audit by the Florida Bar. The problem with random audits is that they are random, and standing alone they will not prevent all misuse or theft of estate or trust funds. But such audits do enhance detection, and they probably have a deterrent effect. Fiduciaries who know they may receive an audit notice may think twice before "borrowing" from the estate or trust account in their hands. But that same Florida case illustrates a recurring problem: lawyers being granted "continuances" on the audit, giving them time to try to cover up the mismanagement of clients' accounts.[6] Such audits should be not only random, they should not be delayed.

A related innovation in lawyer theft detection is mandatory overdraft notification for client trust accounts. Twenty-six states currently have a procedure requiring banks holding lawyers trust accounts "to notify the state lawyer disciplinary agency when those accounts are overdrawn."[7] Unlike random audits, which do require increased funding for state bars, this kind of automatic check on lawyer/fiduciaries requires little in the way of increased funding and seems an easy way to enhance both detection and deterrence.

Educating Consumers of Probate Services
▼

Another important tool in enhancing detection by probate courts is public education about probate law. The more knowledge testators or beneficiaries have about probate, the more likely they will be to contact the court early in the process if a fiduciary is not performing properly. The best defense against a fiduciary who abuses his or her position is a vigilant and well-informed beneficiary who asks questions and takes action before it is too late.

The modern trend toward unsupervised probate assumes the public can protect itself and will know how and when to bring in the court. But this assumption seems to be optimistic in the case of many elderly testators and far-flung beneficiaries. Well-informed beneficiaries and heirs may be the exception rather than the rule. While the new Uniform Trust Code will keep beneficiaries better informed by requiring trustees to make annual reports, this kind of reform standing alone will not create astute, educated beneficiaries who can monitor the fiduciary of the estate or trust at issue.

Public Education or Unauthorized Practice of Law?
▼

The legal profession has not made it easy for the public to become educated about probate or probate avoidance. When Norman Dacey published *How to Avoid Probate* in the 1960s, the New York County

Lawyers Association sued him for the unauthorized practice of law. In 1967, a New York court actually banned the book. The New York Court of Appeals reversed that ban and upheld Dacey's right to give the public knowledge about avoiding probate.[8] The dissent in the intermediate court, which the court of appeals essentially adopted, held that there was no "relationship of personal trust and confidence" because Dacey was selling his book to the general public.[9]

Since the 1960s and the birth of publishing houses like Nolo Press, technology has created new ways to educate the public and assist them in meeting their legal needs. The line between providing information and the unauthorized practice of law is a fine one, especially when it comes to computer software. Although prosecutions for engaging in the unauthorized practice of law waned in the past several decades, there has been a recent resurgence.[10] The Unauthorized Practice of Law (UPL) Committee in Texas has challenged both books and software in its effort to pursue those who claim to educate the public about probate law and assist them in meeting their legal needs. A recent case pitted the committee against Nolo Press.

In 1997, the Texas UPL Committee investigated the allegation that Nolo Press, one of the largest publishers of legal self-help books in the United States, was engaged in the practice of law.[11] The members of the committee are selected by the state supreme court, but its supervisory structure is ambiguous. There are nine committee members appointed by the court, including three nonlawyer members. The committee then authorizes regional subcommittees (generally made up of lawyers who are not committee members) to begin investigations on their own. The allegation that Nolo Press was engaged in the unauthorized practice of law began in Houston, was later moved to Dallas, and was shrouded in secrecy.[12]

The UPL committee sought to have Nolo Press books banned in the State of Texas. The committee's position was that one could only publish a self-help legal book or form book if one had a license to practice law in Texas. A book by anyone, including a lawyer or law professor, who did not hold a license to practice law in Texas, constituted the unauthorized practice of law. Nolo argued that Texas citizens should be free to choose between hiring a lawyer and reading a book and that they knew enough to make the choice. Nolo also argued that the definition of practicing law should have as a prerequisite actually having a client.[13]

In addition to these arguments, counsel for Nolo also stated that the free speech protections of the Texas constitution prohibited banning books in Texas. The committee in essence sought a ban on importing certain books into Texas—a rather drastic and arguably unconstitutional position. The Texas Library Association and the American Association of Law Libraries joined Nolo in its opposition to the committee's attempt to ban the books and software. Several individual Texans who had used Nolo products also joined the suit.[14]

While it may have been Nolo's Living Trusts 2.0 software that precipitated the UPL complaint, all of Nolo's publications were targeted.[15] Nolo Press publishes an extensive list of books addressing all kinds of legal processes. These include books that provide a step-by-step approach for getting through the probate process without a lawyer. They include forms and detailed instructions for filing them in court.

The case ended when the Texas legislature passed a statute that clearly excluded publishing books or selling software from the definition of the "practice of law" in the state of Texas.[16] Pete Kennedy, counsel for Nolo Press, does not believe that the majority of the Texas bar favored banning books or preventing consumers' access to legal information. With its new statute, Texas is now perhaps the most consumer-friendly state in the nation in terms of access to legal publications.[17]

As the Nolo Press case proceeded, there was also an effort to bar the sale of Quicken Family Lawyer.

> In January [1999], Judge Barefoot Sanders of the U.S. District Court for the Northern District of Texas ruled that Iowa-based Parsons Technology, which manufactures Quicken Family Lawyer, engaged in the unauthorized practice of law in Texas by selling the popular interactive software there. The Quicken program allows users to create wills, employment contracts and health-related legal documents by answering questions posed in the software program. Quicken Family Lawyer "goes beyond merely instructing someone on how to fill in a blank form. While no single one of QFL's acts, in and of itself, may constitute the practice of law, taken as a whole, Parsons . . . has

> gone beyond publishing a sample form book with instructions, and has ventured into the unauthorized practice of law."[18]

However, on June 29, 1999, the Fifth Circuit Court of Appeals concluded that after the appeal was filed, "the Texas Legislature [had] enacted an amendment . . . providing that the 'practice of law' does not include the design, creation, publication, distribution, display, or sale . . . [of] computer software, or similar products if the products clearly and conspicuously state that the products are not a substitute for the advice of an attorney.'" The appeals court vacated the judgment and remanded the case to the district court for further proceedings, "in light of the amended statute."[19] Judge Sanders then vacated his injunction as moot, because Quicken Family Lawyer '98 and '99 were no longer being published, and Quicken Family Lawyer 2000 was not the subject of the suit. The UPL committee of the Texas Bar did not refile its complaint.

Halt Legal Tyranny (HALT) is a Washington, D.C.–based organization dedicated to making the legal system more accessible to the public. Their Web site includes a page devoted to legal actions around the country brought by state bars trying to stop publishers and others from engaging in what the bar calls the unauthorized practice of law. However, HALT and others call this an effort to give the public the information it needs to keep the legal profession honest.

Called "The Freedom of Legal Information Project," the HALT effort, "is designed to stimulate and inform public policy debates regarding the right to speak and write about the U.S. legal system and how it functions. This project seeks to reform state court rules and statutes that prohibit the 'unauthorized practice of law' and to expand the alternatives available for legal consumers. Although millions of low and moderate income Americans are priced out of the civil justice system simply because they cannot afford a lawyer, many state bar associations, courts and district attorneys are currently misusing unauthorized practice of law rules to attack inexpensive alternatives to hiring a lawyer, including independent paralegals, legal self-help publishers and volunteers."[20] Cases like those against Nolo Press, Quicken, and others only serve to reinforce the public's perception that the legal profession is less interested in an educated public than in maximizing its fees.

The Legal Profession's Duty to Educate the Public

At a conference in May 1999, a number of speakers emphasized the role of the bar in educating the public. The American Bar Association, the Conference of Chief Justices, the Conference of State Court Administrators, and the League of Women Voters jointly sponsored the National Conference on Public Trust and Confidence in the Justice System in Washington, D.C. The participants began with the "premise that the public's faith in the justice system is in serious need of bolstering."[21] Commenting on the conference, ABA president Philip Anderson stated, "the education of the public is a task for the courts and the bar, and is of much deeper import than a sense that people would like the legal system better if they only knew more about it."[22]

The obligation to educate the public could be a catalyst for greater dissemination of information. The bar should be less protective of the monopoly on the provision of legal services and more concerned with creating knowledgeable clients who ask questions. Some local and state bar associations have responded to this mandate by giving seminars and publishing books to inform the public about probate. The Beverly Hills Bar Association sponsored the book *How to Live—and Die—with California Probate,* a work that offers nonlawyers a succinct and lucid explanation of the probate process.[23] More publications like this, and efforts to provide objective information on Internet bar association Web sites, would go a long way toward educating the public in probate law. In addition, many probate judges, like Judge Mary Sheffield of Phelps County, Missouri, regularly speak to groups of elderly citizens to tell them about the probate process and answer their questions.[24]

There are already many seminars that promise to help the public learn about probate or probate avoidance. Unfortunately, many of them are efforts by lawyers, financial planners, investment advisers, or insurance brokers to persuade people to use their services. There is a great need for unbiased public education about probate. Knowing that there are deadlines and that accounts must be filed annually would help the average trust or estate beneficiary, or the family of an elderly person under guardianship or conservatorship, to ask the right questions of an executor or trustee. If those questions were asked early in the process, they might prevent the kind of fraud or negligence that turns beneficiaries into victims.

The Internet holds great promise for educating the public about probate. With tens of millions of Americans online, bar associations and law schools have an opportunity to broadcast impartial seminars to the public for a minimal fee or for free. These seminars could be pared-down versions of law school classes on wills and trusts and estate administration. More general seminars could teach the public how to choose a lawyer and how effectively to monitor their attorneys.

Lawyers should also be proactive in counseling their clients. They should help their clients to minimize the risk of fiduciary malfeasance by informing them of the variety of estate planning tools that are available. They should educate their clients about the pros and cons of each one. The nonprobate living trust may not be appropriate for a client whose family situation warrants the increased supervision of a third party like the probate court. Lawyers should inform their clients of the benefits of supervision as well as the costs.[25]

Similar offerings on the Internet could help those faced with nominating a fiduciary to choose between their own lawyer, a bank, or a family member. The Web site FiduciaryChoice.com is in the first stages of creating a directory of lawyers and institutions offering their services as fiduciaries. This and similar sites could deliver objective lessons to visitors on comparative fees, the pros and cons of using a lawyer versus a corporate fiduciary, and other information that should be delivered to a client if he is to make an informed decision in choosing a fiduciary.

While there is a fine line between public education and the practice of law, there are many things nonlegal groups can do to educate the public and improve their understanding of the probate process. In addition, the legal profession itself should make greater efforts to inform the public about probate. It should be judicious in choosing its targets to pursue for the unauthorized practice of law. "If we overuse unauthorized practice, the appearance is that all we're trying to do is to protect our monopoly. There is a real danger there. It fosters distrust," says Phil Shuey, who cochaired the ABA Law Practice Management Section Futurist Committee. "The bar should choose challenges carefully and focus on whether the public is being misled."[26]

The probate court is simply a government bureaucracy run by people and is as vulnerable to human frailty as any other system. This will not change. More knowledgeable citizens, improvements in the transfer and availability of information through computerization, random audits, and a more proactive probate court will all help to increase detection and minimize the chance that flaws in the probate system will be exploited by unscrupulous lawyers and fiduciaries.

Chapter 6

Meager Judicial Resources

▼

In order to implement reforms to probate court oversight, such as improvements in technology and audits, states must fully fund their court budgets. The following case tells the story of an underfunded court that let a local lawyer prevaricate and delay until the beneficiaries in some of the cases she handled were left without their bequests and without real recourse.

St. Petersburg lawyer Lauren Sill was the court-appointed personal representative of Joe Thomas' estate.[1] Thomas died in St. Petersburg in 1988 at age eighty-six. His will gave his estate of more than $280,000 to the thirty-two grandnieces and grandnephews he held dear. Sill took charge of the estate and proceeded to steal $270,000 of Thomas' money.[2] It was not as though the court failed to ask Sill to account for the money. Over the years, it asked eleven times, and she failed to answer. The court responded by giving her eleven extensions. Finally, after four years of requests, probate judge Helen Hansel asked a final time. The courtroom exchange went something like this:

"Where's the cash?" demanded Judge Hansel.

"In the bank." Sill answered.

"All $283,000?" asked Hansel.

"That's correct." Sill responded.

A suspicious court employee ran to a phone and called the bank. He quickly returned and said, "Your honor, I have been advised by the Chase Bank that the balance in the estate account at this time is $3,611."[3]

Lauren Sill's legal problems began before her theft from the Thomas estate came to light. A graduate of Stetson University College of Law in St. Petersburg, Sill became a member of the Florida bar in 1981. She embarked on a career path that lead her to become a sort of guardianship assembly line, balancing as many as five hundred guardianships at a time in the mid-1980s.[4] Even when complaints about Sill sparked a criminal investigation and a review by the powerful Florida State Bar, judges in the Pinellas County courts continued to assign her as the attorney in guardianship cases.[5]

Months before the state attorney's office had Sill arrested and charged with grand theft, the state bar had suspended Sill for thirty days due to her mishandling of a family trust.[6] Sill's grandfather, William Krause, died in May 1982. At this time, Sill's grandmother, Eva Krause, had a will that divided her estate equally between Sill's mother and her mother's sister, Eva Joline of Miller Place, New York. Sometime between 1982 and 1985, however, Eva Krause made a new will that gave Eva Joline's half of the estate to Joline's children, Christopher and Bridget, in trust. They were to receive their shares in thirds, at ages twenty-five, thirty, and thirty-five.[7]

The trustee of the Joline children's trust was their cousin, Lauren Sill. Eva Joline did not learn of the change in the will until her mother's death in February 1985. Joline then tried a number of times to learn the terms of the trust and to obtain an accounting from Sill for the trust beneficiaries. After unsuccessful efforts and substantial expense in trying to deal with the Florida courts from her home in New York, Joline hired lawyer Henry Kulakowski of Palm Harbor, Florida, to pursue the case. Kulakowski began his efforts in April 1989, four years after Eva Krause's death. Sill had failed to file any accounts for the trust. Even after a court ruled that Sill must account, she failed to do so. One year and many court orders later, Joline discovered that Sill had used the trust assets for her own benefit.[8]

The legal wrangling continued. Joline had to take time off from work and fly to Florida for meetings and depositions. She had to pay lawyers and professionals $12,000 in fees, and she had to pay court and research costs to prove that Sill had taken her children's money. Finally, after a judge threatened to jail her, Sill produced bank statements showing that she had borrowed $87,500 from the trust, which she had used to pay expenses and taxes.[9]

Sill repaid her cousins' money with interest but was suspended by the Florida Supreme Court on February 4, 1993. The bar accused Sill of "fraud, deceit or misrepresentation reflecting adversely on (her) honesty, trustworthiness or fitness as a lawyer."[10] Sill admitted to a conflict of interest. Later, as Sill was sentenced for grand theft involving a number of other estates, Eva Joline wrote to the court, "I have closely followed the details of Ms. Sill's case. I feel deep empathy for these other people who have been going through the same legal battles as my family did. None of us deserve the psychological anguish or financial loss we've had to endure."[11]

This was not Sill's first encounter with bar discipline. In the early 1980s, the Florida bar had concluded that her behavior merited charges of thirty-three counts of minor misconduct, including procrastination, which she successfully contested, agreeing to a "public reprimand," from the bar.[12] Still, Sill continued to be assigned guardianships. Some people saw her as a good lawyer, someone who took cases that offered little profit but had much merit. Shirley Pence, a former admission coordinator for a 187-bed nursing home, wrote to the court as a character reference on Sill's behalf in January 1994. "I feel the community, especially the elderly has [*sic*] greatly benefitted from the services that [Sill] has rendered. It is not difficult to find an attorney that will represent a private pay ward, but not many will give of their time and resources to see to the needs for [*sic*] the less fortunate. . . . I feel the media has done a great disservice to Ms. Sill, where were the reporters when she was seeing to the needs of a medicaid community that no one else would represent?"[13]

In the Thomas case, Sill was actually appointed by the court. Joseph Thomas was a recreational park director in Buffalo, New York. He was generous to a fault, and every summer would take his dozens of grandnieces and nephews to the neighborhood park where he worked. During the 1950s, he treated the children to annual excursions which they all remembered fondly as they became adults.[14] Uncle Joe, or "Unk" as they called him, retired and left the snowy streets of Buffalo for warmer climes on the west coast of Florida. His will left the estate he had frugally invested and saved to be divided among his thirty-two grandnieces and nephews.

When Thomas died in June 1988, Lauren Sill was named both personal representative and attorney for his estate. She had complete control over the estate's assets and bank account. "The estate originally contained assets in excess of $280,000. All of these assets were in cash, CD's, stock and savings bonds. Over the period of time that Lauren Sill was the personal representative of that estate as well as acting attorney for the estate, [she] made withdrawals payable to herself in an amount in excess of $260,000. There [were] no time sheets, billing records, or any documentation regarding time spent in administration of th[e] estate. . . . There [were no] petitions or orders authorizing any payments of legal fees. . . . There [were] no disbursements made to any of the beneficiaries. . . . as of March 31, 1993, the account that should have been holding assets easily in excess of $250,000 had a balance of $3,611.77."[15]

This account was contained in an affidavit by David Kurash, a well-respected investigator in the Pinellas County state attorney's office. Kurash investigated such other high-profile fraud cases as the financial misdeeds of Henry Lyons, head of the National Baptist Convention. Kurash was put on the case after a spot audit by Florida bar CPA/branch auditor Pedro Pizarro turned up evidence that Sill had taken funds from the estate of Joseph Thomas to replace missing funds in her other client trust accounts.[16]

Kurash's affidavit describes the spot audit. On December 1, 1992, Pizarro went to Sill's St. Petersburg law office to conduct his audit. Sill had received notice of the audit and had asked that it be delayed until December 1. When Pizarro walked in, Sill was there with her lawyer, Peter Giroux of the law office of Edward Foremen, Esq. As Pizarro was getting ready to look at the records, Sill acknowledged that there had been a shortage in the client trust account because of an IRS levy for back taxes. She told Pizarro that the problem had been cleared up and that she had repaid the money to the client accounts. Pizarro asked about the exact date of the repayment, and Sill explained that it was not one date, but, rather, that she had put the money back over a period of time.[17]

Pizarro proceeded to open Sill's books and look at the records. When he was finished, he told Sill that he could not see evidence of any deposit to cover the shortfall. Sill now told him that a check had been deposited the day before (November 30) and that she had the bank receipt to prove it. Pizarro asked for more. Where was the check stub from her law office operating account showing a check drawn on that account to make the deposit reimbursing the client trust account? Sill then admitted the $29,473.30 had not come from her business operating account.[18]

On December 3, 1992, Pizarro and the Florida bar followed up. They had a subpoena served on Chase Bank of Florida, the source of the bank receipt Sill had shown Pizarro. Chase complied and sent copies of the deposit slip and actual check to the bar. The check used to cover the shortfall in Lauren Sill's client trust account had been drawn on the Estate of Joseph J. Thomas, Lauren Sill, personal representative.[19] The Florida bar suspended Sill in April 1993 and later accepted her voluntary resignation with leave to reapply for admission as an attorney after seven years.[20]

In April 1993, the Pinellas County Sheriff's Office executed a search warrant at Sill's office. They seized documents relating to Thomas' estate and Sill's client trust account. Thomas' estate had become the subject of scrutiny by the Criminal Enterprise Division, Economic Crime Section. David Kurash took a close look at the records seized. He pieced together the financial puzzle, revealing a picture of a probate lawyer run amuck. An estate account that should have held at least $250,000 had a balance of less than $4,000. Kurash recommended that the court issue a capias for the crime of grand theft in the first degree, a theft in excess of $100,000, and that Lauren Sill be brought before the criminal court "to answer for these charges."[21]

There were other problems as well. Sill had been the attorney for Oliver Smith, the personal representative of the Germanier estate. Smith had sent Sill a cashier's check for $101,214.51 after he paid all the estate's outstanding bills. Sill had asked him to send the money so that she could distribute it to the heirs, all of whom lived in Switzerland. Sill never sent the money.[22]

Sill was both the personal representative and the attorney for the

Zachry estate. Sill claimed that she had taken $52,875 as "fees paid." The state attorney charged her with theft of those accounts. Sill was the attorney for the personal representative of the Kosanke estate. She wrote checks to herself from the estate that resulted in a charge of theft of $18,605.65. However, there was, "no restitution owed to the Kosanke estate because on October 15, 1992, Sill transferred (stole) $40,000 from the Joseph Thomas Estate; deposited it to her trust account (to make up for the shortage), and then paid all of the Kosanke Estate proceeds to Paul Christenson, the Personal Representative. Christenson subsequently made distribution to the heirs."[23] Again, Lauren Sill had used Joe Thomas' money as her personal credit line.

On December 16, 1993, one year after Pedro Pizarro's spot audit revealed the thefts, Lauren Sill quietly pled guilty to four counts of grand theft.[24] The amount she allegedly stole totaled more than $400,000. While prosecutors asked for a stiffer sentence, Judge Claire Luten settled on two and one-half years in prison for Sill, with a requirement that she provide restitution to the heirs.[25]

Sill's crimes created hardship on the intended beneficiaries of the estates she robbed and created havoc with her own family. At a hearing on March 23, 1994, to reconsider her sentence, Alice Sill, Lauren's mother, made a proposal to the court. She would mortgage Sill's law office, title to which was held in her parents' name, along with other real estate and would offer the Thomas heirs a note for $100,000. But Alice Sill would only agree to help the victims of her daughter's malfeasance if Judge Luten would give her daughter probation rather than jail time. Alice Sill pleaded with the judge, "I really need my daughter at home. My husband was diagnosed in March of 1990 with a serious illness. . . . I also have a twenty-eight-year-old daughter. . . . She is classified as profoundly retarded by HRS. . . . I also have an eighty-nine-year-old mother-in-law who I take care of. . . . I also am responsible for [Lauren Sill's] twins who I love dearly, but they are a responsibility. I take full care of them."[26]

But the judge rejected the offer that State Attorney Glenn Martin characterized as "cash register justice" telling Alice Sill, "Mrs. Sill, I wish to heck there was something I could do personally to help you because you are up to your armpits and there is no getting around that. But I'm also going to be candid with you. There is a reason why all this happened. Whether she gave up her law license voluntarily or not, she would have been disbarred period." The judge then turned to Lauren Sill and said, "Ms. Sill, you stood here earlier at sentencing and you stood here today and your mother is suffering and your children are suffering and do you know, I've yet to see a tear in your eye. You created all this for your parents and to your sister and to your children and to a number of other families."[27] In the end, Judge Luten denied the motion to reconsider Sill's sentence.

Sill served six months in jail and was put on probation in September 1994.[28] Margaret Jendrejzak, a grandniece of Joe Thomas, lamented, "I guess we're never going to get the money back. . . . This is a joke."[29] Another of Thomas' heirs was thirty-year-old Judy Thomas, who "is under a doctor's care. . . . She cannot work. . . . and her SSI from the government leaves her living below the poverty level. . . . Judy lives in very sub-standard housing. . . . She rents a 3rd floor, walk-up on the West-side of Buffalo, N.Y., not a safe area. Peeling paint, leaking roof, bad plumbing, broken-down stove and refrigerator. Broken windows are the norm." Nancy Josa describes her sister Judy as "a kind and simple girl with a heart of gold. She is a loving girl who deserved more in this life, but was dealt a bad hand. And now Ms. Lauren Sill has just slapped her one more time."[30]

Even after a public reprimand by the Florida bar and a number of complaints, the Pinellas County court had appointed Lauren Sill as the personal representative of Joe Thomas' estate. The theme that resonates throughout the victims' statements in the case is that the Florida probate courts share much of the blame for their losses. Sill victim and relative Eva Joline wrote to the court,

> Yes, Lauren Sill pleaded guilty to stealing $421,000 from several estates. But this happened in December, 1993. Isn't it a shame that the legal system kept her in business YEARS after learning she was abusing the very people she was to protect? . . . My faith in our justice system, however, is faltering. I have followed the rules of the Courts. I have paid all the legal fees. I have instilled in my children that justice DOES prevail. And then I look at this case and I say, Why? Why did it take so long to get accountings of the trust funds? Why did it

> take so long to get a new trustee for my children? Why did it take so long to retrieve my children's monies back in their trust funds? Why didn't Ms. Sill have to pay for all our legal fees when she was the guilty party? And then I say further, "Why wasn't she stopped so others didn't have to go through what we did, both psychologically and financially?"[31]

The probate system has no answer for Joline, but many would argue that the courts lack the resources needed to monitor court-appointed fiduciaries. Is this an adequate explanation for the negligence of the probate courts in the Sill matter?

Improving Judges and Court Procedures

▼

Judges are the central actors in the probate process. Long maligned as a less than stellar segment of the American bench, probate judges are the gatekeepers of a process through which as many as a million Americans' estates pass each year. Overwhelmed with cases and plagued by insufficient resources, many probate judges struggle daily against a tide of cases that threatens to drown them. Historically, some probate judges have viewed their position as a perch for dispensing patronage, but many others struggle to bring professionalism to the role and to lobby for increased budgets to do their jobs properly.

Noted probate scholar John Langbein of the Yale Law School has written that "[t]here have long been difficulties in staffing the American probate bench, and some of the people who serve there . . . are menacing."[32] While taking pains to note that competent and devoted judges are readily found in the American probate courts, Langbein makes the point that "the integrity and ability of the American probate bench has so often been found wanting that the confidence in the predictability and correctness of adjudication in these courts has been impaired. Americans can only look with envy to the esteemed and meritocratic chancery bench that conducts probate adjudication in English and Commonwealth jurisdictions."[33]

Langbein's words are part of his review of David Margolick's

Undue Influence, a book describing the notorious Johnson & Johnson will contest in New York City's surrogate's court. Surrogate judge Marie Lambert handled the Johnson case. Langbein quotes Margolick's assertion that, "in New York, Marie Lambert was thought to be especially immune from oversight on account of the perverse financial incentives of the appellate judges. . . . 'the judges of the Appellate Division, her ostensible superiors, went easy on her; once they left the bench, they wanted appointments to guardianships or other lucrative posts that, especially in New York, are treated as patronage plums within the gift of the surrogate."[34]

This political theme was echoed recently when New York's highest judge, Judith Kaye, appointed a "special investigator to look into whether judges favor lawyers with strong political party ties in making lucrative court assignments throughout the state." The chief judge cited the threat to public confidence, "when judicial appointments are based on considerations other than merit."[35] Judge Kaye took action after receiving a candid letter from Brooklyn Democratic Party members who openly complained that they were being excluded from such appointments, "notwithstanding their 'unquestioned loyalty' to the party." The *New York Times* lauded Judge Kaye's efforts to create a "new panel to propose long-range improvements in the fiduciary appointment process" and to examine the "state's system of electing judges, which fosters an unhealthy reliance on party leaders by judges who are supposed to remain above partisan politics."[36]

Other jurisdictions have also addressed the issue of favoritism in probate court appointments. Some courts have tried random assignments of lucrative posts, but in many probate courts appointments are still made at the discretion of the judge, inviting the appearance of cronyism. For example, in Florida, as in other states, "probate judges have the power to dispense not only justice, but lucrative employment opportunities as well. Curatorships or monitor posts can generate up to $100,000 in fees. When these positions are awarded to friends of the judge, the odor of impropriety is unavoidable."[37]

The Dade County Bar Association realized that the public viewed the probate system as rife with cronyism and favoritism. In 1992, the association asked Richard Milstein, a well-respected local lawyer, to study the existing system and propose reforms that would encourage professionalism in probate court appointments. "Although such appointments are often specified in the deceased's will, in many cases a probate judge had discretion to appoint whomever he saw fit. Milstein said frankly: 'Would certain judges favor certain people? Yes. Did it appear improper? Absolutely yes.'"[38]

Milstein's proposal, implemented by the court, created a "probate wheel." The system was designed to make probate appointments "blind," chosen from a list of local lawyers who have registered with the clerk's office. The wheel system built in some discretion. Judges were "allowed to bypass the wheel, if they felt a case required a special skill, such as bilingual abilities, medical knowledge, or complicated asset management." One of Milstein's other suggestions, a tracking system to show which lawyer was appointed and whether the appointment was pro bono or fee-generating, met with the objection that it would be an "administrative nightmare." Flaws in the wheel system thus included lack of scrutiny of the "special" cases that went "off the wheel" and lack of any systematic recording of the appointments made and the fees generated. "There are some people who are being appointed off the wheel more often than others . . . the system is not perfect, he admits. 'We are aware of it. Maybe the wheel needs a bit more inflating.'"[39]

The Move toward Professionalism

▼

In addition to procedural reforms, efforts to professionalize the probate bench are an important step forward. A recent meeting of the National College of Probate Judges was held in the historic Fell's Point neighborhood of Baltimore. The harbor sparkled in the morning light as workmen washed down the cobblestone streets. The police station familiar to Americans as the headquarters of the squad featured in television's *Homicide* stood empty and quiet. On a corner down the street stood the Admiral Fell Inn with its colonial-era brick front and well-appointed lobby full of prints of schooners and grandfather clocks. The dining room was full of probate judges from around the country. At breakfast they sat in groups of two and three, quietly discussing changes in their particular states and comparing their models of probate—supervised and unsupervised.

The historic setting of Fell's Point seemed just right for a meeting of the members of a bench that has existed since the earliest days of the country. These are, however, the faces of a new American probate bench. They are men and women—some appointed, more elected—who see a myriad of contemporary problems as they sit on their benches and listen to cases of family members grappling with an incompetent parent, an adoption gone awry, or a trustee who has failed to account to his or her siblings for their share of their mother's trust. These judges share a common interest in new developments in their field, and a desire to reform the probate system to make it responsive to the needs of the elderly, the incompetent, and the disabled, who rely on their judgment to make critical decisions on their behalf.

The National College of Probate Judges was formed in an effort to professionalize the probate courts and the probate bench.[40] Organized when the probate revolution was in its infancy in 1968, the college, "was established in response to public concern with the time and costs involved in estate administration [and] is the only national organization exclusively dedicated to improving probate law and probate courts." The focus of the college's work is to educate member judges through conferences and seminars and to cooperate with organizations like the National Center for State Courts that are concerned with probate court jurisdiction.[41] The college holds fall and spring educational seminars for probate judges on a variety of topics from elder law, health-care decisionmaking, and adoption to more traditional probate topics.[42]

The college's mission is embodied in ten goals: (1) fostering a court system that provides a more equitable and expeditious administration of estates; (2) supporting the preparation of materials, like court practice manuals, to aid in the administration of the probate courts; (3) helping probate courts apply new technologies to court administration, for example, using computers for document management, court bookkeeping, and fiduciary accounting; (4) cosponsoring seminars for the continuing education of probate judges and court personnel; (5) publishing educational brochures and periodicals; (6) providing educational programs to improve probate administration; (7) cooperating with other organizations to improve judicial administration; (8) serving as a research and learning resource for judges and scholars studying probate administration; (9) assisting in drafting probate legislation; and (10) encouraging, where applicable, the preparation and adoption of standardized uniform practices, both within and between states.[43]

At their Baltimore meeting in March 2000, a roomful of judges listened as A. Frank Johns, president of the National Academy of Elder Law Attorneys, spoke about changes in practice and ethical rules that loomed as a challenge, and perhaps a threat, to lawyers representing the elderly. Johns honed in on the ethical issues presented by the new model of "multidisciplinary practice." This method of serving clients would provide "one stop shopping" for accounting, insurance, and legal services. Johns reviewed the risks that might arise as a result for judges who routinely have cases of vulnerable, elderly citizens before them.[44] This kind of effort to connect probate judges to the practicing bar, and to keep them informed of the multitude of social and legal changes that affect their day to day work, is a model of a more professional probate bench.

This new professionalism extends as well to other segments of the probate world. A new legal speciality, "elder law," takes a holistic approach to the many issues that can affect the elderly client—medical, socioeconomic, and legal. Issues, such as medical advances that provide a new understanding of the functioning of the human brain, touch upon areas probate judges must integrate into their difficult decisions each day. Demographic changes have yielded a growing elderly population, which will continue to put pressure on probate courts in ways that scholars, judges, and practitioners are only beginning to analyze and discuss. The complex matrix of medical, demographic, legal, and social issues that make up elder law is clearly important to the American probate system and its bench. The National College's efforts to educate probate judges have gone a long way toward nurturing a more professional and responsive probate judiciary.

The Effort to Standardize Practices

▼

Another focus of the National College is encouraging probate courts around the country to adopt model rules and standards. Uniform procedures and rules would make probate law work better for the increasingly mobile society of the United States. Historically, there have been major differences in probate procedures not only from state to state, but from county to county within a state. The National College polled forty-two of its state representatives, and an "overwhelming number of respondents stated that current standards . . . do not sufficiently address the concerns of probate courts." The majority of those responding to the poll noted that "national probate standards were needed in the areas of fees and commissions, court automation, judicial education, judicial officers and support staff, and financial and fund management, and to address the performance of courts exercising probate jurisdiction."[45]

The college responded to this call for a uniform, professional approach to probate court management by joining with the National Center for State Courts to produce a set of national standards for probate courts. The project was supported by a grant from the State Justice Institute, with a supplemental grant from the American College of Trust and Estate Counsel Foundation. The goal of the standards, which were approved in 1993, is "to provide a common language to facilitate description, classification, and communication of probate court activities; and, most importantly, a management and planning tool for self-assessment and self-improvement of courts throughout the country exercising probate jurisdiction."[46]

One of the National Probate Court Standards focuses on caseflow management. Standard 2.2 "recognizes that the court with probate jurisdiction . . . faces a heavy caseload that it must process expeditiously, yet fairly."[47] Studies have reported that active management of cases "is the single technique responsible for the success in reducing delays" in the courts.[48] The National Probate Court Standards advocate automated case management systems and prior timetables for cases to move them as quickly as possible through the system.[49]

The standards require each court to develop a caseflow management system to reduce backlogs and improve the efficient disposition of cases, while allowing for early identification of difficult cases that may need more time or cases that need to be addressed immediately.[50] They also recommend status conferences early in the case to define the time the case will require. Status reports should be the norm, creating a record to show whether timelines are being honored.[51] Many probate judges around the country have adopted these kinds of new case management techniques, expediting the probate process and making it more efficient and accountable.

Judicial Funding

The explanation that courts most frequently offer when a case of fiduciary misconduct hits the front page is lack of judicial resources. It is easy, court personnel say, to blame the courts, but if society wants a well-oiled judicial system, it has to provide the cash to run one. Funding for probate and other courts varies widely from state to state. In some states, funding comes from the state, and in others, local governments like counties fund the courts. But in all states, there is a cry for more money if the public expects the administration of justice to improve.

In a perfect world, there would be adequate salaries to attract and keep capable judges and "court personnel, supplies, equipment, and library materials; to purchase specialized services such as those provided by court visitors, physicians, psychologists, expert witnesses, examiners, and consultants; and to obtain, renovate and replace, where needed, capital items and physical facilities such as courthouses, courtrooms, offices and courtroom and office furnishings."[52] Given the variety of functions the probate court performs, protecting the elderly and minors, tracking assets and creditors, and realizing a decedent's final wishes, it is clear that an efficient and effective court must have a fully funded budget.

In the aftermath of the Gunderson case in California, described in

Chapter 3, one commentator stated, "The problem is that there is already little time for judges or examiners to check for suspected wrongdoing given the number of cases pending in probate courts and the volume of trusts that are created . . . registering all durable powers of attorney with the court to have them reviewed would create an enormous burden and an expensive bureaucracy."[53]

Unfortunately, no national database details the volume or composition of pending probate court cases. The National College of Probate Judges has identified this dearth of statistical data and has noted that "Caseload statistics are the single best way to describe the courts' current activities, as well as to predict what they will likely face in the future. Caseload statistics are analogous to the financial information used by the private sector to organize their operations. Well-documented caseload statistics provide powerful evidence for claims for needed resources."[54]

Courts must appeal to the legislature to get their fair share of the budgetary pie. In a 1989 conference on a project by the Institute for Court Management (within the National Center for State Courts) in cooperation with the National Conference of State Legislatures, the author of the project report identified court funding as a critical issue and described a commission established in Arizona created to study the issue. "The Arizona Commission noted [the] inadequacy of court facilities and [the] inability of courts to meet the demands created by new legislation."[55] This echoes the California State Bar's comments in the Gunderson case. The probate court's failure to identify the problems in Gunderson's files as they moved through the probate process might have been solved by a more thorough court review of each file, but this mandate comes with a price.

Some politicians have identified inadequate trial court funding "as one of the reasons for the public's loss of respect for the judicial system."[56] In September 1991, a funding crisis led the chief judge of the New York Court of Appeals and the chief administrator for the Courts of New York to file a lawsuit against the governor and the legislature aimed at securing more funding for the beleaguered courts of New York. As the chief administrator described the crisis, "Not long ago the ability of the courts to provide . . . access was severely impaired. Ten years of chronic underfunding of the courts culminated with a cut in the court system's budget that brought the courts below the level necessary to function adequately. And people knew it without having to see the budget numbers. It was apparent from the decrepit courthouses, poor ventilation and acoustics, long lines, and stories of judges leaving the bench for other employment. It was evident in the increasing delays in cases, curtailed hours of services, closed courts, and news accounts of "revolving door justice."[57]

One of the difficulties in garnering public support for court funding is the perception of government waste that permeates public discourse. New York's chief administrator for the courts argued that "The importance of adequate courthouses that inspire respect for the law and confidence in the government's ability to provide justice cannot be overstated."[58] But the public's vision of profligate spending by governments in general and courts in particular is reinforced by news reports like the one in June 1997 describing a call, "for an audit of Los Angeles County courtroom construction projects because more than $80 million has been spent on eight proposed courthouses without a single courtroom being built."[59]

Groups like the National College of Probate Judges, and individual probate judges around the country, have effectively advocated for enhanced court budgets. The National Probate Court Standards emphasize the importance of judicial leadership in advocating for increased probate court funding and in administering these funds in a professional manner. With increased financial resources, probate courts can implement reforms to improve oversight through better caseflow management, random audits of trust and estate accounts, comprehensive computerization of records, increased court personnel to review records, and innovative uses of the Internet. Reforms like these might have made a difference in cases like Fairbanks, Biegen, Gunderson, and Sill. While increased court budgets might not have stopped those lawyers from abusing their fiduciary duties, better probate court monitoring might have raised red flags and put a halt to their behavior far sooner.

The American probate bench has long suffered from the public view that it is the least capable segment of the American judiciary and is, at worst, actively corrupt. Groups like the National College of Probate Judges, the National Center for State Courts, and the American College of Trust and Estates Counsel have made significant strides in educating the probate bench and advocating for uniform standards and laws, all essential elements of probate reform.

Chapter 7

A Conspiracy of Silence

▼

One of the lessons of the cases discussed in previous chapters is that better funded courts might have picked up the malfeasance earlier. Unfortunately, full funding of court budgets is not likely to come any time soon. In a recent *Business Week* article, the authors note that "Even when the economy recovers, state budgets could be wrecked by a nasty mix of anemic revenues and exploding health-care costs into the foreseeable future."[1] This puts more pressure on other lawyers in the community to detect unethical behavior by lawyers and fiduciaries. But in the Fairbanks, Biegen, Gunderson, and Sill cases lawyer misconduct went on for years, with little or no response by other professionals who were or should have been aware of it. One product of this silence is the cost borne by the victims, beneficiaries, or wards who would have been protected had someone had the courage to speak up earlier.

In the Sill case, for example, a commentator criticized the system saying, "It's not as if the judges, Bar and prosecutors didn't have ample warning that something was wrong in many of Sill's cases. . . . The judges expressed their deep concern, then gave Sill more cases."[2] This pattern of silence was also pervasive in the Fairbanks case. Witness after witness testified to the legislative committee that people knew what was going on, but were afraid to report Fairbanks' misconduct. In some cases, they had tolerated his evasions in their own courtrooms and were complicit by their silence. The Florida legislative report highlighted the cozy atmosphere of the courthouse, and one probate victim remarked, "The people who are supposed to uphold the trust are more geared to their personal networks. . . . It isn't a system of checks and balances. It's more like a good ol' boy network."[3]

What is the legal profession's approach to "whistleblowing" among its members? Prior to 1983, the American Bar Association had its Model Code of Professional Responsibility, and many states adopted its Rule 1-103(A). That rule provided that "A lawyer possessing unprivileged knowledge of a violation of [a Disciplinary Rule] shall report such knowledge to . . . [the] authority empowered to investigate or act upon such violation."[4] In 1983, the code was replaced by the Model Rules of Professional Conduct. Rule 8.3 took the place of Rule 1-103(A). Rule 8.3(a) provides that "a lawyer who knows that another lawyer has committed a violation of the rules of professional conduct that raises a substantial question as to that lawyer's honesty, trustworthiness or fitness as a lawyer in other respects, shall inform the appropriate professional authority."[5]

These rules emphasize the duty of a lawyer, an officer of the court, to report wrongdoing by others in the system, be they lawyers or judges. These goals are laudable, but there is clearly a tension between working smoothly with one's fellow lawyers every day and turning one of them in for unethical or illegal conduct. Aside from a natural unwillingness to bring sanctions on one's friends, there is the equally human reluctance to rock the boat. Courts are much like other governmental bureaucracies, one needs to "go along to get along." Successfully representing a client requires being able to navigate the judicial system effectively. This means knowing and trading favors with the bureaucrats who manage the system, judges, court clerks, and other lawyers. Reporting on a member of the system may result in his dismissal, but those who remain may not treat the whistleblower with great kindness afterward. This can impair a lawyer's livelihood and her ability to represent her clients effectively.

While lawyers may have an ethical mandate to report wrongdoing, they rarely do so. Even rarer is a partner turning in another partner for unethical behavior. The aversion to "ratting" is compounded by the fear that there may be general financial responsibility for the misbehavior of one's partner. A notable exception to the conspiracy of silence can be found among the lawyers of the State of Illinois. In 1988, the Illinois Supreme Court disciplined a lawyer, James Himmel, for failing to report that another lawyer had committed a theft. The court suspended Himmel from the practice of law. Himmel "became the only lawyer in U.S. history to be disciplined solely for not blowing the whistle."[6]

According to Justice Stamos, who wrote the opinion in *In re Himmel,* the story began in October 1978 when Tammy Forsberg was injured in a motorcycle accident. Like many accident victims, Forsberg retained an attorney, John R. Casey, to deal with the insurance company and to negotiate a settlement on her behalf. Casey was successful in obtaining a $35,000 settlement offer from the insurance company and, as is the custom, he was supposed to receive one-third of the settlement as his contingency fee.[7]

The insurance company sent a check directly to Casey in March, 1981. Casey cashed the check, deposited it to his client's trust fund account and then promptly took the entire $35,000 for himself. After Casey converted the money, Tammy Forsberg kept trying to collect the $23,233.34 that belonged to her. In March 1983, Forsberg hired a second lawyer, James H. Himmel, to keep up the pressure on Casey to ante up the cash. Of course, Forsberg had to agree to pay Himmel a fee. They agreed on one-third of any amount above $23,233.34.[8]

James Himmel soon discovered that Casey had misappropriated the $35,000. Himmel drafted an agreement between Forsberg and Casey in which Forsberg agreed to forgo any criminal, civil or attorney disciplinary action against Casey in exchange for his paying her $75,000. Casey jumped at the chance to avoid being reported for his conversion of client funds and he signed the agreement on April 11, 1993.[9]

As one might expect from someone who converted the original check, Casey did not pay up. Finally, in February 1985, James Himmel sued John Casey for breach of the settlement agreement, obtaining a $100,000 judgment against Casey for Tammy Forsberg. Himmel would have received a $25,000 fee if he could have collected the $100,000 judgment. However, all Tammy Forsberg ever collected from John Casey was $5,000 before retaining Himmel and $10,400 after hiring him. Himmel never received any fee for his work on behalf of Tammy Forsberg.[10]

The Illinois Administrator of the Attorney Registration and Disciplinary Commission filed a complaint to have Casey suspended from the practice of law in April 1985. Casey was disbarred by consent in November of that year. Although he knew of Casey's defalcation, Himmel had never reported him to the bar disciplinary authorities. Thus, after going after Casey, the administrator filed a complaint against Himmel for violating Rule 1-103(a) of the Illinois Code of Professional Responsibility. That rule, like Disciplinary Rule 1-103(A) of the ABA Model Code of Professional Responsibility on which it was based, required attorneys to report other attorneys' misconduct when they became aware of it. Himmel's defense was that his knowledge of Casey's misconduct was protected by the attorney-client relationship; it was privileged information that he could not reveal without violating other parts of the code.[11]

On October 15, 1986, a bar hearing board rejected Himmel's defense and recommended that he be reprimanded. The case proceeded to the next level, where the review board agreed with Himmel and, on July 9, 1987, they recommended dismissing the complaint against him. The Illinois Supreme Court then took up the matter, and on September 22, 1988, issued an opinion concluding that Himmel should have reported the Casey theft to the bar, and that Himmel should be suspended from the practice of law for one year.[12]

In the year following the Himmel decision, the Illinois Attorney Registration and Disciplinary Commission received 922 complaints by lawyers against other lawyers. These included complaints from some old-line law firms that, historically, might have fired a partner quietly and sought reimbursement, but who never would have turned in one of their own. One of Chicago's most prestigious firms, Winston & Strawn, reported the firm's former managing partner, Gary Fairchild. Fairchild was subsequently convicted of cheating both the firm and his clients out of $800,000. He lost his license to practice and received a two-year prison sentence.[13]

The American Bar Association included a rule requiring attorney whistleblowing in its first Code of Ethics in 1908. "Lawyers should expose without fear or favor dishonest or corrupt colleagues." A 1974 survey of Boston lawyers indicated, however, that only 6 percent would turn in a colleague for misconduct. Those who opposed this approach objected to the irony of lawyers, who are supposed to guard their clients' confidences at all costs, being forced to reveal potentially privileged information. They also feared misuse of the rule as leverage in negotiations. The Illinois Supreme Court subsequently issued a rule prohibiting the threat of a Himmel complaint in negotiations, but lawyers are aware that Himmel possibilities can subtly affect negotiations.[14]

Massachusetts provides an illustration of how difficult and divisive this issue is for the legal profession. In 1996, the Massachusetts Supreme Judicial Court's Committee on the Model Rules of Professional Conduct "recommended a new rule that lawyers 'should' report the disciplinary violations of other lawyers—declining to propose a mandatory 'shall' requirement." At the time, Massachusetts had no reporting rule at all. The proposed rule provoked strong reactions. Attorney Mark D. Immerman of Northampton said, "I'm against a mandatory reporting requirement. It would feed an adversarial relationship between attorneys which is already strained due to competition and would diminish collegiality that is already in a downward mode." Peter J. Carrozza of North Andover was also opposed, saying, "We shouldn't police ourselves in situations like this. Our duty is we should individually conduct ourselves according to rules and regulations of professional conduct. We should not be responsible for the actions of other attorneys. We have the Board of Bar Overseers to handle such matters."[15]

There were also Massachusetts attorneys like Cynthia Bauman of Boston, who said, "I support a rule that lawyers should report disciplinary violations, [but I] think that the SJC committee's recommendation not to use the word 'shall' is something that I agree with. I think that some degree of discretion is important because the circumstances of each case may differ greatly." Some argued that if such a rule were enacted, it should be accompanied by immunity from civil liability for those attorneys who did report the misconduct of a another lawyer.[16]

If a "whistleblower" ethics rule is to be discretionary, then the public must trust that lawyers are well trained in ethics and will actually report serious lapses by their colleagues. But are lawyers really equipped to exercise such discretion wisely?

Teaching Young Lawyers about Ethics

Over the past several decades, bar associations have integrated ethics training into their continuing legal education programs. A parallel process has occurred in the legal academy, and law schools have begun to reevaluate the training they offer their students. Were they teaching them to be ethical practitioners of the legal arts?

In his article, "Teaching Ethics Seriously: Legal Ethics as the Most Important Subject in Law School," Professor Russell Pearce of Fordham details the history of ethics teaching in American law schools.[17] Citing noted legal ethics scholar and Stanford law professor Deborah Rhode, he writes, "During the early twentieth century such instruction remained quite minimal, usually consisting of lecture series by judges or prominent attorneys. For many of these series, no credit and no grade were given. . . . In the 1950s, leaders of the Association of American Law Schools recommended that law schools offer both ethics courses and pervasive teaching of ethics throughout the curriculum. At the same time, the reality of law school teaching contradicted this aspiration. A survey revealed that most ethics courses 'consisted of only one hour of ungraded instruction each week' and that very few, if any, non-ethics courses included pervasive ethics instruction."[18]

The Watergate scandal in 1974 and the decline in the status of the legal profession should have sparked a greater interest in teaching ethics, but most offerings were still perceived as "low status." Pearce cites Roger Cramton and Susan Koniak when he notes that even though high-level scholarship and innovative casebooks and teaching methods have arrived on the scene, "in most law schools today legal ethics occupies a minor academic role as a one-or two-credit required course in the upper-class years, often taught by adjuncts or by a rotating group of faculty conscripts."[19]

According to Pearce, the second-class status of legal ethics in the law school curriculum is "the product of three powerfully entrenched perspectives: (1) a faith in the ethical guarantees of professionalism and the methods of legal education; (2) the belief in the scientific basis of legal education; and (3) the assumption that adults lack the capacity for ethical development." Pearce argues that legal academics often simply rely on the general character building functions of legal education to turn out ethical graduates and that such academics have a misplaced faith in the ability of the profession to police itself. "Indeed, the mounting evidence of unethical lawyer conduct continues to prompt demands for improved ethics teaching by law schools."[20]

Most states require students to pass the Multistate Professional Responsibility Exam, a multiple-choice test, which measures a student's familiarity with the ethical rules that govern law practice.[21] Some believe that students, who often take this test during their third year of law school, view learning ethics as simply memorizing a set of rules.[22] There has long been a belief that because law students are adults, their ethical constructs are fully formed before they come to law school. Some scholars contend, however, that "while law students have well-formed personal values stemming from family, church, and society, they nonetheless have relatively unsophisticated and unformed ideas of what it means to be a 'good lawyer'."[23] Pearce notes that "more than one hundred studies of moral education courses found that 'well-designed' curricula can significantly improve capacities of moral reasoning."[24] Whether legal ethics education has been effective is unclear, but Deborah Rhode has said, "There is . . . more evidence on the effectiveness of professional responsibility instruction than there is on the effectiveness of most professional education."[25]

Other law professors, like Jeffrey Pennell at Emory, have made the point that ethics training in areas like estate planning and administration is not an abstract, philosophical matter. Some ethical rules and guidelines are procedural and specific and do not rely on the "moral character" of the law student to be absorbed.[26] Thus, many believe that ethics training can be effective in preventing lawyers from abusing their positions of trust. But are students being generally well served by the institution that the public expects to train lawyers in ethics and their professional responsibilities—the American law school?

In his article, "Legal Ethics in Decline: the Elite Law Firm, the Elite Law School and the Moral Formation of the Novice Attorney," law professor Patrick Schiltz notes that law firms have given up mentoring young lawyers due to financial pressures, and that law schools suffer from a related lack of mentoring. Schiltz outlines three major conditions that must exist for effective mentoring to take place. Along with ethics training, Schiltz argues that mentoring is a primary source of ethical training in legal academia. He suggests that (1) the academy must accept the idea that one of its primary functions is to train students to practice law and to do so ethically; (2) every faculty must include a substantial number of professors who have practiced law or who have a "genuine interest in the work of practitioners and judges"; and (3) faculty members must spend time with students outside the classroom for effective mentoring to take place.[27]

Schiltz and a number of other scholars have argued that the disproportionate emphasis on publishing rather than teaching has resulted in a dearth of mentoring in law school. He characterizes this imbalance as "academic greed," with a focus on "the accumulation of academic prestige rather than material wealth, and it is measured in pages published rather than hours billed."[28] This echoes the "intellectual schizophrenia" described by law professor Thomas Bergin in his 1968 article "The Law Teacher: A Man Divided Against Himself," in which he describes the law professor as "a man divided against himself," the victim of an "intellectual schizophrenia" that has him "devoutly believing he could be an 'authentic academic' and a trainer of practitioners."[29]

Schiltz says what many legal academics already know but do not want to concede, that the primary road to tenure, research money, and lateral moves to more prestigious law schools is the number of articles published, not the quality of one's teaching.[30] As Schiltz says of tenure, "one's teaching will not even factor into the decision unless it is so bad as to provoke student rioting (and that may not even be disqualifying)." Other faculty benefits like merit pay increases, sabbaticals, and research leaves also depend on publishing. Schiltz concludes that the legal academy's greed for prestige is "claiming mentoring and in a larger sense, the ethical practice of law as its victims."[31]

Perhaps this "research university" model works at "elite" law schools like Yale or Harvard where most graduates go into teaching or practice in large law firms. But the graduates of the "elite" schools will move into large firms with sophisticated corporate clients who are capable of monitoring their attorneys. The graduates of the nation's less prestigious schools will tend toward "retail" law practice, in small firms or solo practice settings. Since many lawyers involved in the probate process as attorneys for the estate or as fiduciaries practice alone or in small firms, they lack the large-firm oversight structure that tends to minimize the risk to clients. Law schools and law professors therefore play a direct role in guarding the public's interest. They are all that stands between a client and an incompetent novice attorney. The burden on them to train young lawyers in the skills necessary to carry out their duties in the profession is enormous.

In the end, law schools are professional schools. They exist to train lawyers. While legal scholarship is an important function of law schools, it should be balanced with other important missions. Law schools must offer incentives to make classroom presentations more effective. They should think critically about the law school curriculum as a better tool for training competent and ethical lawyers. Some legal scholars have proposed remedies to the structural deficiencies that plague the current "dualist" model of legal education. They have offered new visions for legal education that would provide a diversity of approaches. These might, for example, allow faculty to gravitate to what they do best, with some teaching and some writing, thus improving the quality of both.[32] Such an approach would encourage and reward faculty who want to spend time with students that those students require to become competent lawyers. As Professor Schiltz argues, "Law professors can mentor and thereby shape students into ethical people who will practice law ethically. But before they can do so, they must first regard professional training not as something done grudgingly to pay the bills, but as a worthy endeavor in itself. That attitude seems to be on the wane among law professors today."[33]

The begrudging attitude described by Schiltz is in part a result of who makes up the faculties at American law schools. The public, which directly and indirectly supports legal education through tax dollars and federal loan subsidies to law students, would be surprised to discover that "Forty percent of the nation's law professors in ABA law schools have no private practice experience. The mean is only 2.5 years of private practice experience. Only five percent have ever been partners." In addition, law faculties have strikingly similar pedigrees. "Approximately one-third of all law professors graduated from just five of the 'top' law schools, while sixty percent of law professors went to the 'top' twenty 'producer' schools."[34]

Critics of modern legal education like Manuel Ramos, have made the point that while "Law professors disdain lawyers whose pure pursuit of profit makes a mockery of any ethical or competence standards . . . most law professors continue to send ill-prepared lawyers into the profession . . . and allow their law schools to serve as incubators for legal malpractice." Professor Ramos links the increase in legal malpractice to high tuition costs (up to $120,000 for three years of law school) and heavy student debt loads. "A lawyer's relentless pursuit of profit is increasingly, in part, a result of legal education's indifference to escalating tuition costs, and its inability to change tired, decades-old courses and professors. Young lawyers join the overgrowing ranks of solo practitioners who already make up over half of the lawyers in private practice. They are increasingly incompetent, and, unfortunately for their clients, uninsured, and still adept at hiding their assets." With the median income for lawyers at only $40,000, there is pressure to take on additional clients.[35] That pressure is an ever-present ethical challenge for young lawyers.

Teaching Students to be Competent Fiduciaries

The standard law school curriculum is largely focused on training students to become zealous advocates. Lawyers are seen as a vehicle for their client's wishes and law schools emphasize the lawyer as advocate before a court, a government agency, or a similar body. Ethics scholar

Geoffrey Hazard of the University of Pennsylvania has described the traditional advocacy role of lawyers: "A lawyer is an agent, not a principal. Having taken on a client, a lawyer is not free to pursue the client's objectives only to the extent that the lawyer may see fit. The lawyer has to go forward to the point that the client sees fit, within the limits of the law."[36]

However, the role of the lawyer as executor, trustee, or guardian, as opposed to that of zealous advocate, requires the lawyer herself to decide on objectives. Often, the client in these fiduciary situations cannot make these decisions since he is dead, a minor or incompetent. Without training in decision making, the lawyer as fiduciary is at sea—lacking the confidence and experience needed to make an appropriate decision based on the critical analysis of the facts that she was trained to make in law school.

One of the structural problems is that law schools still teach in large part through the case method, introduced by Christopher Columbus Langdell at the Harvard Law School in the nineteenth century.[37] Since students must parse appellate cases, this method puts students in the mind-set of appellant or appellee, winner or loser. This contrasts with the role of a fiduciary, who may well be playing a more representative role in dealing with deceased clients, minors or incompetent adults. The case method does little to train students to move beyond a critical analysis of the facts and a formulation of the issues, to the next step of deciding how to make an informed judgment and act on it. Lawyers usually turn to their clients at this critical juncture and ask them how they want to proceed. In contrast, fiduciaries often cannot ask their clients and must make decisions on their behalf, using a substituted judgment model of decision making.

A more profound structural flaw in legal education is law schools' failure to teach that lawyers are fiduciaries, a concept as old as the profession itself. Every time a lawyer takes on a client, he enters into a general fiduciary relationship with that client. Property, torts, contracts, civil procedure, and criminal law professors struggle to indoctrinate their new students in the fundamental theories of law with little attention to the general role of the lawyer as fiduciary. Few of the courses in the law school curriculum go over the rules governing fiduciaries or consider the theories that inform their actions. The concept of "fiduciary duty" is relegated to brief mentions in wills & trusts, corporations, and, perhaps, professional responsibility or contracts courses. Other courses that might be useful to lawyers who act as "statutory" fiduciaries, executors, trustees, or guardians are not typically offered. For example, courses that cover topics like the portfolio theory of investing and financial concepts like diversification are all but absent from the law school curriculum, as are courses in the psychology of the elderly, although more schools are adding elder law courses as electives. Discussions of estate administration are relegated to a chapter or two in the basic wills & trusts casebook. It is difficult to find a casebook to teach a course in estate administration or to find a law school that offers a course dedicated to the specifics of this important process.

Fred Miller, former executive director of the New York Lawyers Fund for Client Protection calls upon "law schools or bar examiners to test students for competency to be a fiduciary."[38] Given the experience of the New York Fund that 60 percent of claims against the fund are "estate-related defalcations,"[39] such a demand is completely understandable. American law schools should carefully consider curricular reform that introduces young lawyers to the duties and responsibilities of the fiduciary role. With the growth of the elderly population, and the increase in the legal dilemmas that require lawyers to act as fiduciaries, the challenge for American legal education in the twenty-first century will be to move beyond the skills students are traditionally taught, critical analysis of facts and the formulation of legal theories, to develop another skill, the ability to take information as a fiduciary and use it to act competently and ethically on behalf of a client.

More lawyers need to have the courage to report their colleagues for serious ethical lapses. American legal education reform, with an increased emphasis on ethics and fiduciary duties, should increase the number of lawyers who are familiar with and who embrace the duty to report a colleague's misconduct. That new generation of lawyers would, in turn, increase the number of states that eventually follow the Himmel example. Few states have yet done so, perhaps fearing the negative consequences of the rule. And in Illinois, while the rule has increased the number of lawyer-to-lawyer complaints dramatically, few attorneys have actually been disciplined for simply failing to report a colleague's wrongdoing.[40] The problem is that without such a rule threatening lawyers with loss of their licenses for failing to report wrongdoing, the incentives to not report tend to prevail in individual cases. State by state, there are few lawyer-to-lawyer complaints. In the case of Virginia lawyer David Murray, described in the next chapter, there were at least a dozen lawyers who seemed to know he was embezzling millions of dollars in client funds but who failed to stop him.[41] Would lawyers following the rule set down in the Himmel case have made a difference in one of the biggest lawyer theft cases in American history?

Chapter 8

An Inadequate Safety Net

There are those who would endorse exclusive reliance on post-facto remedies as the best approach to further reforming probate. Such observers would retain the noninterventionist approach to probate courts embodied in the Uniform Probate Code and the Uniform Trust Code, as well as trust fiduciary bonds, state client protection funds, and liability insurance to compensate parties who suffer as a result of the lack of oversight by the probate court. While appealing in principle, the current safety net available to compensate the victims of bad lawyers and fiduciaries has rather large holes in it. The following case illustrates some of those holes.

The U.S. Park Service ranger spotted the car on a February morning in 1992. It was parked by the side of a road along North Carolina's picturesque Outer Banks. The ranger's initial inspection indicated that the neatly dressed driver had a .357 Magnum revolver and a can of Budweiser next to him as he apparently lay sleeping. The ranger called for backup from sheriff's deputies. When they arrived and opened the car door, the occupant did not wake up. In fact, he was dead. He had been shot twice, once through the ribcage and the second time through his sternum. The medical examiner who performed the autopsy concluded that David Murray, member of a prestigious Virginia legal family, had killed himself after consuming enough alcohol to register 1.5 times the legal limit. Murray committed suicide just one day after the FBI raided his office. They were investigating allegations that he had stolen $42 million in client funds.[1]

David Murray had created a Ponzi scheme, built in large part on the two things his father had left him, his reputation for trustworthiness and an enormous real estate empire in southeastern Virginia.[2] When the real estate market took a dive, Murray could not pay the high returns he had promised his investor/clients.[3] So Murray dipped into estates entrusted to him, stealing about $4 million.[4]

David Murray was the son of a prominent Newport News attorney, Philip Murray. The elder Murray, a member of the state legislature and the head of the local school board for many years, was considered one of the city's finest lawyers.[5] Philip Murray founded the bank that came to be known as NationsBank, now part of the mega-institution Bank of America. The Murray family also invested heavily in real estate, "from Williamsburg to the waters of Hampton Roads."[6] Philip Murray used his real estate holdings to secure investments he made on behalf of his clients. The elder Murray had begun the family tradition of venturing beyond traditional law practice into financial investing for clients, promising and delivering high returns for thirty years. David Murray inherited his father's land and the penchant for investing, but not his father's luck in delivering returns.[7]

In the 1980s David Murray tried to develop residential communities on much of the land he had inherited from his father.[8] One of Murray's close friends, Newport News vice mayor William Fitzgerald, said that his wife Joyce, "was one of 75 people who invested nearly $5.5 million in a housing development Murray promoted in James City County. She turned over $15,000 that she had inherited from her mother, Fitzgerald said."[9]

Murray also set up another company, Virginia Telco Ltd., to raise cash. He convinced seventy-five people to invest more than $2.7 million. Murray's investors ranged from the most prominent citizens of Newport News to elderly retirees on pensions. And why not? David Murray had promised his investors up to a 24 percent return on their money. Who would fail to invest in such a great deal, especially given Philip Murray's long track record of delivering high yields? The friends, family, and clients who turned over money to David Murray trusted him completely. Virginia Telco Ltd. was sold to these investors on the promise that Murray was in line to get a lucrative contract for supplying pay phones on military bases. Murray did not get the contract, but that did not stop him from continuing to solicit funds and to promise high returns from the deal. A subsequent federal investigation showed that Murray had personally guaranteed some investors' money.[10] In a letter dated November 1989, Murray wrote to a Telco investor, "You naturally seem concerned about the risk. . . . I will personally guarantee your investment by a note to you."[11] The investor never received anything as a return on his share.

As the real estate market sank, Murray's "residential properties went deeper and deeper into debt."[12] As his need for cash increased, Murray stooped ever lower on the fraud ladder. He sold twenty different investors a one-half share in a North Carolina restaurant ($150,000 each). He claimed he had a buyer ready to take over the restaurant and that the sale would net more than $25,000 in profit. Murray raised more than $1 million this way, but it was not enough. He had to dip into trust funds and estates to keep his scheme going. In January 1992, Murray admitted that he had used $1.7 million in an estate and trust in his charge to bail out his own land deals.[13] It was a classic breach of fiduciary duty. A tip from the Virginia State Bar about the trust matter sent the FBI to Murray's office on February 6, 1992. The FBI raid and the impending collapse of his personal and professional worlds sent Murray off to Nags Head in a rented Buick to commit suicide the next day.[14]

The investigation that followed Murray's death revealed that he left behind at least $41 million in debts owed to more than four hundred clients and investors. According to the ABA, Murray's financial swindle was one of the largest by a lawyer in U.S. history. In the end, few of his clients saw any of the money he had stolen, but even then, his friends wanted to believe the best about him. One friend who never recovered a $100,000 loan said, "No one will ever convince me that he was a crook. It's just that what he did was crooked."[15]

The purpose of probate is to provide oversight, but all the oversight in the world did not seem to help David Murray's clients. The Virginia courts provide a commissioner of accounts to review probate accounts filed by fiduciaries. These commissioners are appointed by the circuit courts to examine estate accounts on an annual basis.

Henry Mullins III was the Newport News commissioner of accounts who reviewed Murray's actions. He resigned in the wake of the Murray scandal. Some newspapers quoted "authorities" as saying Mullins, "could have moved to stop at least one of Murray's schemes in January 1991, but he failed to do so."[16] There were plenty of red flags. Murray "missed dozens of deadlines to document his handling of inheritances he had sworn to safeguard."[17]

Murray's investors and clients were not his only victims. In the federal bankruptcy proceedings that followed Murray's death, his wife testified that she had no knowledge of her husband's financial dealings. Anne Murray filed for Chapter 11 bankruptcy following her husband's death. She also testified, as she tried to fight foreclosure proceedings on her modest home in Newport News, that David Murray had forged her signature on documents that deeded away a large portion of her property. She received nothing from her husband's estate. David Murray's son and legal associate, David M. Murray Jr., pleaded guilty in August 1993 to one count of conspiring with his father to defraud the Farmer's Home Administration. He had previously been disbarred. Assistant U.S. attorney Harvey L. Bryant said that Murray took the money to keep his father from financial ruin.[18] His father left him a bitter legacy.

The people Murray victimized took one novel step as they searched for compensation for their losses. They filed an action against the Justices of the Virginia Supreme Court and Virginia State Bar officials under federal civil rights laws, the Racketeer Influenced and Corrupt Organizations Act (RICO) and the Freedom of Information Act. Their complaint asserted that their constitutional rights were violated by the conduct of "state actors" because these actors failed to protect the public from the fraudulent activities of David M. Murray. Murray's victims further argued that the justices of the Virginia Supreme Court should have better regulated the practice of law and sanctioned Murray for his behavior. The victims argued that the state bar should have brought disciplinary actions against Murray and that it violated the victims' rights by denying or reducing their claims against the client protection fund.[19]

On December 21, 1994, the Federal District Court for the Eastern

District of Virginia dismissed the victims' action for lack of jurisdiction and failure to state a claim.[20] Murray's victims had exhausted all sources of relief within the legal framework set up to protect people like them. As it turns out, that framework contained some very large holes.

The Virginia Bar's Response

"There's nothing like the theft of more than $40 million by one lawyer to get an integrated bar to focus on the philosophical and practical aspects of the bar's responsibility for its dishonest colleagues." So wrote the *National Law Journal* about the Murray scandal in 1993. The Virginia bar responded to the Murray case by appointing a special committee to investigate the matter and propose reforms. The committee's role was to "deter and prevent theft in the first instance, detect it quickly, purge the profession of dishonest practitioners, and provide compensation for the victims."[21] After the Murray case, this was quite a tall order.

The Special Committee on Lawyers Serving as Fiduciaries reported to the Council of the Virginia State Bar on June 1, 1993. Its report was subtitled, "Recommendations in Favor of a Program of Random Reviews." The committee acknowledged that "It is inescapable that most lawyers do not even know what the requirements . . . are for the maintenance of their firm's trust accounts. This problem existed before David M. Murray, Sr. Now, after the Murray . . . case, how can the bar ignore what appears to be widespread ignorance of the record keeping rules promulgated by the Court?"[22]

The special committee concluded that an important mechanism for monitoring lawyers serving as personal representatives, trustees, or guardians was the random audit. The committee cited nine other states with such a procedure in place. Delaware, Iowa, Nebraska, New Hampshire, New Jersey, New York, North Carolina, Vermont, and Washington all "have a program of random verification of lawyer trust accounts."[23] The committee members chose the New Jersey model as the one to recommend to Virginia and noted that the New Jersey program had uncovered thirty-five cases of misappropriation since its inception.

As for the chances that such a program would have deterred David Murray, the committee analogized to IRS audits. "What cannot be denied is that the possibility of an IRS audit enhances voluntary taxpayer compliance in this country, and that the discipline of accountings to a Commissioner of Accounts has both deterrence and early detection advantages." The committee acknowledged that if it failed to act there would be public demands for other remedies. "If the Bar does not deal with the problem as presently perceived by the public, surely the public will find someone who will. Will the public be better served by rules that may discourage lawyers from serving as fiduciaries, either by a requirement of mandatory bonding or otherwise? . . . The commitment of resources to a program for reviewing lawyer trust accounts would be merely an extension of the Bar's role as the Court's investigator and regulator of persons already licensed to practice law. The need is there. The time has come."[24]

Speaking of the financial resources needed to prevent another Murray case, the committee chair echoed a familiar refrain, "Effective systems of deterrence cost money, whether they are random audits of trust accounts, a tighter system of regulating fiduciaries, or eliminating the general practice here of drafting wills that waive surety for executors."[25] The Judicial Council of Virginia also promised to "establish a subcommittee to work on improving the state's commissioners of accounts system." As the *Virginian-Pilot* reported in March, 1993, the Newport News commissioner of accounts, Henry G. Mullins, "did not hold Murray to requirements demanded by state law during a period of time stretching back to the early 1980s."[26]

The Virginia bar's executive committee went on to adopt many of the committee's recommendations. In addition, they considered improving the client security fund, and they increased bar dues by fifteen dollars to make a modest move in that direction.[27] Client protection funds are clearly an important piece of the compensatory safety net for the victims of probate misconduct.

The Safety Net

When an executor or trustee mismanages or steals money entrusted to him, heirs or beneficiaries may take several paths to obtain compensation. They can sue the executor or trustee for breach of fiduciary duty, looking for damages (perhaps from a bonding company if a bond were required). They can sue for malpractice if the damages are the result of negligence. Or they can seek restitution from the state's client protection fund if there has been an outright theft. Victims can also complain to the state bar and its disciplinary body. The problem with this course of action is that if the case is not big enough, it may not be investigated. And if the bar determines that the lawyer should be disciplined, there is no monetary compensation to the victim. Discipline may stop the lawyer from harming other clients, but by itself it will not put money back into the pockets of the victims of attorney negligence or outright theft.

Many laypeople are unaware that if a lawyer acts as an investment advisor and loses the monies invested, legal malpractice insurance and state client reimbursement funds are not available to compensate the injured clients. The fact that someone has a law degree and is a member of the bar does not mean that he or she is always acting as a "lawyer." If the project that a lawyer promised would yield a 24 percent rate of return goes belly up and if he actually invested the money in the promised project, there is no recourse. If the lawyer failed to put the money in the designated project, he may be guilty of criminal fraud and liable civilly. But the protections afforded clients in an attorney-client relationship are not available if the activity involved is investing for the client rather than acting as the client's lawyer.

If a lawyer is "judgment proof" and has few or no assets, and if no bond or insufficient bond was required, a malpractice case may be the only way to tap a "deep pocket." But there are obstacles to this remedy as well. The first is that it is often difficult to find a lawyer to sue another lawyer. The second is that, in most states, many lawyers do not carry malpractice insurance. As a result, the client may win but never collect any cash. In California, 55 percent of the state's forty-five thousand lawyers are not insured.[28] Finally, clients may turn to state client protection funds, but most of these are significantly underfunded. The American probate system requires a secure safety net to compensate the victims of the process.

Breach of Fiduciary Duty and Posting Bond

The first element in the safety net for probate clients is the requirement that fiduciaries post bond. However, it is common practice for courts to waive bond in probate cases, especially if the testator has explicitly waived the bond requirement in his or her will. Waivers are intended to save estates money, but a bond costs only pennies per dollar of estate assets covered. If the probate courts had required bonds covering the assets in the cases detailed in this book, the victims would have recovered more of their losses without having to bring sometimes futile malpractice lawsuits or requesting reimbursement from state client protection funds. For example, in an estate from which Lauren Sill stole $270,000, each of the thirty-two beneficiaries "could have had bond protection for $30 a year."[29]

Given the confidential relationship between lawyer and client, and the risk of uninformed consent in waiving bond in a will, courts should consider requiring bonds in all cases that pose a significant risk of conflicts of interest or risk of loss. This might include, for example, cases where lawyers are nominated as fiduciaries in instruments they draft or are appointed by the court as administrators. Bond should only be waived when the lawyer presents proof that she carries a sufficient fiduciary bond or liability insurance to cover the estate assets.

The ABA Council of the Section of Real Property, Probate and Trust Law suggests in the second of its "Principles for Attorneys Acting in Other Fiduciary Roles" that "The attorney acting as an executor, trustee or other fiduciary should carry a fiduciary bond or liability insurance in an appropriate amount for purposes of protecting the estate, trust or other account and its beneficiaries from any misappropriation or misapplication of fiduciary funds or other insurable loss." The council's desire that lawyer/fiduciaries adequately protect against malfeasance was strong enough that it urged the ABA to "study the possibility of providing such fiduciary bond or fiduciary liability insurance on a group basis to attorneys."[30] The council suggested linking this insurance program to the establishment of "bar-related audit activity" for trusts and estates in the hands of lawyer/fiduciaries.

There are some courts that are addressing this issue, in some cases requiring that a non–family member attorney have proof of at least $250,000 of liability insurance or requiring attorney/fiduciaries to file bonds.[31] The trend is slow but there is some indication that the high-profile cases of fiduciary abuse on the nation's front pages are having an impact on probate courts and judges.

Malpractice Insurance

▼

The second element in the safety net when a lawyer is the fiduciary is malpractice insurance. A probate system that required bonds unless the fiduciary showed proof of liability insurance would provide a deep pocket for the potential victims of fiduciary misconduct. The legal profession could also consider making malpractice insurance mandatory. It would seem to be a logical step to make malpractice insurance a prerequisite to practicing law, but only Oregon has done so, though Illinois may soon follow.[32] Oregon has a state-run insurance pool, the Professional Liability Fund, which is the nation's only mandatory legal malpractice insurance program. A few states do not require lawyers to carry malpractice insurance, but mandate that those lawyers disclose this fact to their clients.[33]

Lawyers and law professors have advocated improving bar disciplinary practices as the solution to the few bad apples that they say plague any profession. But a few others have argued that disciplinary boards are an ineffective and inefficient means of regulating lawyers in the public interest. These commentators have suggested abolishing state disciplinary boards and simply letting malpractice litigation be the tool for regulating lawyers. Their argument is that the $4 billion a year in legal malpractice claims paid each year dwarfs the annual budgets of all the nation's lawyer-discipline systems put together; only $100 million is spent annually on lawyer discipline. Manuel Ramos, successful plaintiffs' attorney turned law professor, argues strongly for abolishing the lawyer discipline system, requiring mandatory malpractice insurance as a more effective means of protecting the public from an epidemic of negligence.[34]

Ramos also notes the dearth of courses in American law schools focusing on malpractice. While there has been a boom in ethics courses, only Tulane and a handful of other schools actually offer seminars on legal malpractice. Students are presumably supposed to absorb the concepts through their ethics training. Ramos argues that is not happening. He notes that most classes contain no discussions of bad or negligent lawyering. Certainly there are few that assign cases involving malpractice.[35]

Mandatory malpractice insurance is common in other countries.[36] As one advocate for mandatory malpractice in the state of Texas argued, "Each attorney in Canada, England, Ireland, Australia and the state of Oregon is required to carry certain minimum limits of professional liability insurance. . . . Any person in [Texas] who attempts to transfer title to a car, purchase license plates, or drive on state highways is required to purchase minimum limits of liability insurance. . . . Approximately 60 percent of the attorneys in private practice in [Texas] have no professional liability insurance. . . . [They] either do not have the assets or the inclination (or both) to compensate clients whom they damage. . . . Attorneys are professionals and owe a fiduciary duty to their clients. . . . It extends to not causing harm to their clients."[37]

However, there are those within the American legal profession who argue that mandatory malpractice coverage is a bad idea. Ramos cites Harry Schneider, former chair of the ABA's Standing Committee on Lawyers Professional Liability: "There is no reliable data documenting that legal malpractice is a widespread phenomenon. . . . Mandatory malpractice insurance effectively defers to the insurer . . . who will . . . be permitted to practice law. . . . Premiums surely will rise across the board as all acceptable risks are pooled automatically with those who otherwise would be considered high-risk lawyers. . . . Additionally, announcing publicly the availability of funds to pay claims will tend to increase the frequency of malpractice claims, frivolous and otherwise."[38] The argument that it would encourage a flood of litigation may or may not be true. But given the fact that there are mechanisms for handling frivolous litigation, it should not end the discussion of whether requiring malpractice insurance is a good idea. Letting attorneys obtain a license to practice law while "going bare" in terms of insurance only seems to bolster the public's perception that the profession does not care about the victims of its worst members.

Unfortunately, there has not been much support for the idea of mandatory malpractice insurance. "Ironically, in the late 1970s, California, one of the most egregious states when it comes to uninsured lawyers, passed a mandatory legal malpractice insurance law, but the governor vetoed it. Oregon borrowed the proposed California legislation and passed it as its own. Lester Rawls, the Oregon Professional Liability Fund's (PLF) former CEO, explains why Oregon had a significant number of uninsured lawyers: 'About 35 percent of our attorneys were not covered by any insurance at all. . . . It wasn't because they couldn't afford it, they just didn't want to pay for it. 'The public be damned' they'd say. Our bar association didn't think that was an appropriate position."[39]

Oregon not only requires malpractice insurance, they provide it. In partial response to the insurance crisis of the mid-1970s, Oregon created a state-subsidized insurance provider that provides the mandatory insurance to Oregon's lawyers. The 1995 assessment for Oregon's lawyers was $2,100. The $2,100 premium purchases a no-deductible policy that provides the required $300,000. An attorney can buy another $700,000 for $1,175, hardly excessive and presumably deductible as a business expense. Each attorney in Oregon pays the same premium, and the premium is only adjusted upward by a 10 percent surcharge if an actual claim is filed. Each year there is a 13 percent chance of having a claim filed against an Oregon lawyer. The average cost to the PLF for both indemnity and defense costs has been a mere $16,000. While in 1993, the PLF showed a loss of $1.4 million with 701 claims made, it showed a projected net income of $789,865.[40]

Young lawyers faced with crushing debt (the average law student graduates with more than $50,000 in loans to repay) might argue that they cannot afford one more payment.[41] Law schools seem quite comfortable imposing an enormous financial barrier to entry for those who want to practice law. If a student cannot come up with between $10,000 and $25,000 per year for tuition, she will not be able to graduate and take the bar exam. If law schools can profit from enormous student debt, the public is entitled to say that those wishing to practice law should have to come up with $2,000 or $3,000 per year for malpractice insurance. Perhaps the bar should provide loans for those lawyers who cannot otherwise afford the premium, much like the federally subsidized student loans to law students that provide a large proportion of the operating budgets of most American law schools.

Most of the public would agree that if the profession is to stave off legislative regulation by arguing that law is a profession, not just a business, what better way to do so than by requiring financial protection of clients in order to maintain a license. Such an argument also distinguishes the practice of law from those businesses regulated by a state's consumer affairs agency.[42]

Ramos is critical of those academics who claim that malpractice litigation alone is an inadequate remedy for aggrieved clients. He notes that Geoffrey Hazard of the University of Pennsylvania Law School has argued that malpractice is only practical for open and shut cases or those with substantial damages.[43] Deborah Rhode of Stanford Law School cites, "the costs, the difficulties of proof, the insufficient assets of uninsured lawyers, and the minor damage claims as reasons why legal malpractice as a form of regulation is 'inadequate'."[44] Who is right? Well, for the victims of negligent and fraudulent probate lawyers, the answer has little practical value. But if those lawyers who had been given fiduciary responsibility had been insured, their victims might have been able to recover something.

Malpractice insurance, however, often excludes intentional misconduct like theft and may contain exclusions for those acting as fiduciaries, making mandatory bond, fiduciary liability insurance, and adequately funded state client protection funds even more important. Since malpractice policies may have exclusions for intentional misconduct or acting in a role other than lawyer, mandatory malpractice insurance may not be as comprehensive a method for ensuring that money is available for victims as would a system of mandatory bond or fiduciary liability insurance. But mandatory malpractice, or at least disclosure, would contribute to mending some of the holes in the safety net.[45]

State Client Protection Funds

▼

The third and final element in the safety net is a state client protection fund. These funds are often woefully underfunded and only pay after all other remedies have been exhausted. Some critics have argued that such funds are little more than window dressing for the state bars, complaining that the existence of client protection funds makes it appear as if the bar is providing for the victims of lawyer theft. But there is actually little money to pay those victims who have often lost tens if not hundreds of thousands of dollars. In several of the cases herein, victims were partially compensated by such funds, but often left far short of complete restitution.

When the victims of David Murray's scams began to get wind that they had been swindled, they turned to the Virginia State Bar's Client Protection Fund for help. Like many states, the Virginia bar had established a fund to help the victims of the profession's worst lawyers. When the Murray clients looked to the fund in 1992, it contained only $580,000, not nearly enough to satisfy the tens of millions of dollars in potential claims. The accountant assigned to straighten out the Murray estate sent more than four hundred claim forms to people who felt that Murray owed them money.[46] However, many of those claims were from people for whom Murray had acted as a financial adviser rather than a lawyer, an activity not covered by the state client protection fund.[47]

"Typically, reimbursement is limited to losses occurring within a client-lawyer relationship or when the lawyer is serving in a fiduciary capacity."[48] The client must have suffered a loss due to the lawyer's dishonest conduct. So such funds are not available to reimburse clients for negligence or malpractice. To obtain redress for these acts of malfeasance, the client has to sue. In addition, the Virginia fund provided that claimants with a net worth of more than $1 million or an adjusted gross income of more than $75,000 in the year preceding the claim were not eligible for reimbursement for their losses.[49] Thus, many of Murray's victims would never see their money again.

Client protection funds are a relatively new phenomenon, and there has been much discussion in the legal literature about their efficacy. Are they serious attempts to create a pool of money to help the victims of the worst of our profession, or are they merely window dressing? These funds exist in forty-nine states and the District of Columbia.[50] They are usually funded with a fee levied on the members of a state's bar association. The ABA Model Code of Professional Responsibility states that "Contribution to a client's security fund is an acceptable method of meeting a lawyer's obligation . . . to participate in collective efforts of the bar to reimburse persons who have lost money or property as a result of the misappropriation or defalcation of another lawyer."[51]

Lawyers are the only professional group that has set up such a mechanism to help victims of unscrupulous members of its profession. These funds originated during the early twentieth century when English Commonwealth countries instituted programs to compensate victims of lawyer theft. Vermont became the first U.S. state to set up a client protection fund in 1959. Within the American Bar Association, there is a Standing Committee on Client Protection, which established an Advisory Committee on Lawyers' Funds for Client Protection. That committee published a 1993–95 survey on client protection funds that detailed such issues as "new fund implementation, fund management, funding sources, reimbursement activities, claims experience and procedures, public information initiatives, loss prevention activities and records management information."[52]

According to a 1998 article in the ABA publication *Professional Lawyer,* client protection funds have approximately $43 million in reserve. While the goal is to reimburse every victim of a bad lawyer, "because of funding issues, the volume of claims filed, the size of the claims and other factors, most United States jurisdictions have placed limits on the maximum allowable reimbursement per claim or per accused lawyer. According to the 1993–1995 Survey, the average maximum limit per claimant is $43,533, the average limit per claim is $43,644, and the average cumulative limit per lawyer is $132,292. Only Connecticut, Delaware, Massachusetts and Montana are without reimbursement limits."[53]

In 1995, the *Connecticut Law Tribune* ran an article on lawyer theft. The *Tribune* asserted that claims of such theft and mishandling of money were on the rise. "Some incidents are outright stealing; others involve lawyers who dip into client funds, thinking they can pay the money back; in other cases, lawyers take fees and never perform the work." There had been a "run" on the Connecticut Client Security Fund, and the amount of claims was clearly higher than the value of the fund. Other states have seen a similar rise in claims, with New York reporting claims in excess of $25 million each year between 1991 and 1994. The directors of state client protection funds could not pinpoint whether lawyers were actually stealing more or whether citizens were more aware of their rights and simply filing more claims.[54]

In 1991, the number of claims against the Connecticut fund was up to forty-three from twenty-three the previous year. "A few states have experienced steady growth in claims against lawyers. In Massachusetts, the Client Security Board awarded $147,000 in 1989. In 1994, that number reached $1.2 million. In Florida in 1984–85, 142 claims were filed against 186 lawyers. . . . The areas of practice hardest hit by thefts haven't changed greatly. Many claims arise out of real estate transactions, personal-injury settlements and appointments as trustees for estates."[55]

States vary dramatically in their payouts as well. "According to a 1993 study by the American Bar Association, Florida's fund was the second slowest in the nation in paying claims. . . . To appreciate how badly Florida's legal community treats its victims, consider a similar program in New Jersey. While Florida takes a year to 18 months to pay most claims, New Jersey takes six months. While Florida pays a maximum of $50,000 per claim (and often much less), New Jersey pays up to $200,000. The key to New Jersey's success—and Florida's failure—is money. And not a lot of money. In New Jersey, most lawyers contribute $50 a year to the victims' fund. In Florida, by contrast, each lawyer chips in only $11. Starved for cash, the Florida fund relies on a hard-working but tiny staff and the lawyers who serve as volunteer investigators."[56]

Still, in each of 1993, 1994, and 1995, over $36 million was paid out to victims of bad lawyers, with thefts in the area of estates and trusts accounting for a large number of claims. "Client protection funds are one of the legal profession's best kept secrets. It is perhaps predictable that the public is largely unaware of the existence of such funds. . . . Delaware did not pay any claims for the years 1993, 1994 and 1995. Historically, many fund trustees and administrators have been reluctant to publicize their activities for fear that there will be a "run on the fund" or that announcements of large pay outs will cause the public to generalize the bad acts of a few to the vast majority of lawyers who faithfully and honestly serve their clients."[57] However, Illinois, New York, New Jersey, Maryland, Massachusetts, Ohio, and Pennsylvania regularly announce payments from their funds to the public. California, the District of Columbia, Maryland, New York, Pennsylvania, and Tennessee run public service announcements to notify the public that the funds exist. Even lawyers are, for the most part, unaware that these funds exist and some are reluctant to pay to fund them. On the whole, however, there is a general recognition that since lawyers have a monopoly on practicing law, they should be and have been obligated to protect clients from the inevitable bad apples in the profession.[58] It is the right thing to do, and it is also good for the public's perception of the profession.

Should lawyers pay increased dues to provide better funding for state client protection funds? Increasing dues by $100 per year hardly seems a burden on lawyers, especially in a country that does not require them to carry a minimum amount of malpractice insurance. In a country with almost one million lawyers, that adds up to at least $100 million per year, a significant increase over the approximately $48 million currently on reserve.

There is evidence that many of the claims against state client protection funds result from probate matters. "According to the 1995 Annual Report of the Lawyers' Fund for Client Protection of the State of

New York, estate-related defalcations by attorneys account for 60 percent of all claims made against the fund."[59] It can be argued that the negligence of the state's probate courts in cases like Fairbanks, Biegen, and Sill allowed the victims to suffer such severe damage. The probate court's granting of multiple extensions of time to lawyer/fiduciaries who failed to comply with accounting requirements or court orders to report on the status of a case allowed those lawyers to continue their misconduct. The result was increased loss to the heirs and beneficiaries.

Since the probate courts bear some responsibility for the public's losses, state legislatures should consider subsidizing claims against state client protection funds to compensate those members of the public who have suffered a loss as a direct result of a dilatory probate court. Such payments might be deducted from a probate court's budget, much as public schools are now being financially sanctioned for not meeting performance goals.

Combined with procedural changes that encourage probate courts to be more proactive in cases that pose significant risk of conflicts of interest, state subsidies of client protection funds would provide an incentive for probate courts to act unilaterally to protect elderly clients and beneficiaries from the few lawyer/fiduciaries who abuse their trust. Mandating that the state make up the difference between the amount that a victim loses and the amount available to pay that victim from a state client protection fund and deducting it from a probate court's annual budget would provide an incentive for probate courts to improve court procedures and oversight of probate matters.

Requiring mandatory bond, implementing a system of mandatory fiduciary liability insurance for lawyer/fiduciaries (or extending mandatory malpractice insurance to all states), and improving the funding of state client protection funds will provide a more seamless web of compensation for parties who suffer as a result of probate court inaction or fiduciary theft. Each of these reforms costs money but is essential if the probate court is to fulfill its mandate to protect the elderly, the incompetent, and the deceased.

Chapter 9

A Failure of Character or Discipline?

The cases in this book involve lawyers who were executors and trustees. There are also nonlawyer fiduciaries who negligently lose or intentionally steal estate or trust funds, and some of the reforms proposed in the previous chapters would minimize the risk of loss in such cases. But while the legal profession can only affect nonlawyer behavior through broad procedural change and better court funding, there are more specific ways it can regulate members of the bar who are involved in probate. Lawyers pervade the probate process in a variety of roles, including serving as the lawyers for nonlawyer executors or trustees. How does the profession regulate the ethical quality and behavior of its members, and can it do so more effectively?

Most states require applicants for the bar exam to have graduated from a law school accredited by the American Bar Association. There are fewer than two hundred of those schools in the United States. According to Deborah Rhode, "In the vast majority of accredited law schools, character plays some role in admissions determinations. A 1970 poll revealed that eighty-five percent of administrators at those institutions believed character qualifications were relevant in the assessment of applicants. All but six current admissions applications have some questions concerning character."[1] This concern for character screening comes in large part from state bar requirements that applicants must undergo some sort of character evaluation before their admission to the bar. The first step in many states is for the dean of the graduate's law school to certify to the bar that the student is of "good moral character."

Richard Zitrin and Carol Langford, in their book *The Moral Compass of the American Lawyer,* theorize that the shift in the law "from profession to business, and the corollary subordination of ordinary moral and ethical concerns to financial ones" is central to understanding the cases of lawyer misconduct that seem to blaze across the headlines today.[2] This shift is echoed in law professor Patrick Schiltz's work when he describes the resultant decline in mentoring.[3]

This sea change in mentoring and the loss of a fiduciary sensibility on the part of older lawyers is one in a complex kaleidoscope of factors that lead to lawyer misconduct. Greed, both financial and professional, is often the model to which young lawyers are exposed as they begin developing the professional habits of a lifetime. But is it simply greed that leads lawyers to breach their fiduciary duty? Other explanations like situational ethics and addiction have also been offered to explain these failings.

There are those who argue that people are neither "good" nor "bad." Rather, they behave differently given different sets of circumstances. Richard Brust describes this "situational ethics" view in the legal arena, labeling the trend in lawyer thefts as the "robbing Peter to pay Paul" syndrome. These lawyers are mostly, "mid-career men with family responsibilities and lifestyles to maintain. They tend to practice in small or solo practices, many of which are struggling to survive in a tight economy. Those practices frequently lack the internal bureaucracies and auditing controls governing larger law firms."[4]

Brust too cites "the bottom-line business-intensive nature of current legal practice combined with an overabundance of high-achieving lawyers struggling to make ends meet" as one of several reasons for lawyer theft. The need for lawyers to produce more paperwork to comply with increasing regulation and increasing malpractice fees has added to small practitioners' fixed costs and consequently to the pressure when fees run dry. In addition, the stress from a cash flow problem may lead lawyers to substance abuse which makes the problem worse. Many of these lawyers are in their late thirties, forties, or fifties—the "crunch years" when private school tuition, bigger houses, and college costs all combine to put lifestyle pressure on the lawyer's practice. "There are a few who are crooks, but with the vast majority who have problems with converting money, generally there's a direct link to some other problem. . . . I've seen one or two who classify as criminals as opposed to attorneys who have problems that lead them to do things wrong."[5]

According to the lawyers for many fiduciaries who are caught stealing from estates and trusts, their failures are not moral or ethical failures but rather stem from addiction, much like people who spend every dime of their social security checks on the slot machines in Atlantic City and cannot afford to lose.[6] Addiction—to gambling, alcohol, or drugs—is a frequently cited reason for lawyer theft. The legal profession is beginning to come to grips with the fact that many of its members grapple with drug and alcohol abuse and suffer from a number of compulsive behavior problems that affect their ability to provide competent legal services to clients. Not only can such addictions result in incompetence, but they can also trigger outright criminal behavior in some lawyers. When lawyers are also executors or trustees, they have even more opportunities to engage in such behavior, since they have full legal control of the assets of an estate or trust. The opportunity for mismanagement or theft is pervasive in these cases. The mix of addiction with the power of a such a lawyer is explosive in terms of the damage that can be done to beneficiaries.

The Texas bar's approach to chemical dependency and mental health issues offers a comprehensive approach to the problem that could be a model for other states. In Texas, the Board of Law Examiners may require an applicant for law school or the bar "to submit to a licensed treatment facility for a chemical dependency evaluation" if there is information that indicates they have such a problem. Legislation in 1991 made changes to the admissions process that now make a license to practice law "probationary" for two years. The board has to make a finding that the person applying for admission is free of the problem before recommending the state supreme court grant him or her a permanent license.[7]

This attempt to identify chemical dependency problems early and to monitor applicants who suffer from them is a valuable tool in protecting the public from the unethical behavior that may result from such dependence. The Texas legislation allows the bar to put conditions related to rehabilitation and recovery on the chemically dependent licensee. For example, "abstinence from alcohol and controlled substances for two years, regular and consistent participation in a recovery support group, regular and consistent attendance at a peer group for lawyers recovering from chemical dependency, regular reports submitted to the board, and the appointment of an attorney monitor who has at least weekly contact with the monitored attorney and who submits monthly monitor reports to the board. The monitor may require the attorney to submit to random drug screens."[8]

This sort of intervention at the front end of a lawyer's career may well prevent her from engaging in unethical or criminal conduct somewhere down the line. The public benefits by such up-front screening, although such programs clearly impinge on the rights of the applicant in terms of privacy, especially when extended to mental health issues. The bar in each state has to balance costs and benefits and decide what best serves the public while not overreaching in terms of the applicant's rights.

While some lawyers have problems before becoming lawyers and the Texas model provides for intervention to address these lawyers and their problems, many lawyers develop addictions later on in their professional lives. The ABA Commission on Lawyer Assistance programs and its Model Lawyer Assistance Program prototype, described later in this chapter, has been effective in expanding such programs to all fifty states.[9]

For example, the Wisconsin Lawyers Assistance Program addresses a comprehensive range of problems from drug abuse to gambling addictions. "The program consists of a committee of attorneys who oversee the program; two helping professionals who are available by phone 24 hours a day, seven days a week; and a brigade of volunteers all around the state who can be called upon to help a fellow attorney one-on-one." In order to encourage lawyers to avail themselves of the program's services, the committee operates on a completely confidential basis. Their "focus is on prevention—before someone gets in too deep."[10] This kind of intervention might prevent some lawyers from hiding their addictions for a long time and minimize the damage to clients and beneficiaries.

Other state bars have also begun to address this problem. For example, Massachusetts has an organization called Lawyers Concerned for Lawyers. The group operates independently from the bar. The organization works cooperatively with the Supreme Judicial Court, the Board of Bar Overseers, and state and local bar associations. Funding comes from an annual assessment included in a lawyer's registration fee. Lawyers Concerned for Lawyers is essentially a confidential counseling and referral service for lawyers, judges, and law students, as well as their families. Its philosophy is that "Lawyers are not unique. Millions of Americans suffer from depression, anxiety, and other health problems. Millions more struggle with alcohol and drug dependency. Many are legal professionals who find their careers and families slipping away as they grow more desperate." The organization appeals to lawyers in trouble to contact them, emphasizing that they do not have to try to solve their problems alone: "There is no need to risk your license, livelihood, reputation, or family." They encourage lawyers to call if they are aware of other lawyers who are suffering from addiction. "By calling us, you may be doing the lawyer a lifesaving favor."[11] That may well have been literally true in the case of a David Murray or a John Fairbanks who took their own lives after their crimes came to light.

The efficacy of state lawyer assistance programs varies and funding such programs requires a commitment from state bars that is often lacking. But given statistics like those generated by an ABA survey in California and New York that indicated "50–70 percent of all disciplinary cases involved alcoholism," the profession as a whole must address this problem.[12]

The studies on attorney impairment also indicate an unwillingness among lawyers to report the misconduct of their fellow lawyers, misconduct that may well be a result of addiction. A recent *ABA Journal* article suggests that if a lawyer learns that another lawyer is using illegal drugs, there may be more than a duty to report to a lawyer assistance committee. There may be a duty to report such misconduct to the bar disciplinary authorities for investigation. As the author put it,

"The truth must have ethical consequences."[13] This reluctance to enforce the "whistleblowing" rules of the profession must be addressed if cases of lawyer/fiduciary abuse are to be curbed.

There is a lack of uniform and comprehensive data on the link between substance abuse, alcoholism or other addictions, and lawyer theft. But it is obvious that "untreated, impaired lawyers" are disproportionately the subject of malpractice and discipline cases. Many of those writing about this problem in the profession agree that "The diseases of alcoholism and drug abuse have devastating effects upon the legal profession and are major factors in the loss of public trust. Afflicted lawyers are unable to practice law in a competent manner and in accordance with professional rules of conduct. The result is that the majority of lawyer-discipline cases involve alcoholism or chemical dependency. Lawyers who remain untreated probably will become subjects of disciplinary investigations."[14]

Not only do such impaired lawyers represent a disproportionate percentage of those engaging in misconduct, but compared to the general population, lawyers are also disproportionately addicted. "It is generally accepted that 10 percent of the adults in the United States chronically abuse alcohol. This percentage does not seem to apply to lawyers. In fact, the percentage is much higher for attorneys. A Washington study found that '18 percent of lawyers who practiced 2 to 20 years had developed a problem drinking, [and the number increases to] 25 percent [among] lawyers who practice 20 years or more.'"[15]

In 1988, the ABA created the Commission on Impaired Attorneys. Its goal was to explore the issue of lawyers addicted to alcohol and drugs and those with mental health problems. The ABA also adopted the Model Lawyer Assistance Program in 1985 to set up a prototype for states interested in helping such lawyers. The Commission on Impaired Attorneys was renamed the Commission on Lawyer Assistance Programs in 1996, so that the public's understanding of its work would include the educational function of the commission as well as its role as a source of innovative ideas about facilitating recovery. As recently as 1980, only twenty-six state bars had lawyer assistance programs, but that number has grown to include all fifty states.[16] Like Lawyers Concerned for Lawyers, these programs include counseling, referrals to recovery programs, and methods to intervene and assist impaired lawyers.

In cases of addiction and misconduct, it is often not just the lawyer who is in denial about his or her problem, it is also the other lawyers who practice and come in contact with the attorney who is engaging in misconduct. That silence compounds the damage to the victims in these cases. "The symptom of denial is not limited to the alcoholic. It appears to be evident in the reluctance of many lawyers and judges to report impaired or incompetent colleagues. This institutional denial is an obvious violation of the obligation to report impairment or incompetence under the Model Code and the Model Rules. Described as the 'conspiracy of silence' it may be the 'greatest obstacle to better regulation of the legal profession.'"[17]

Lawyer assistance programs help those lawyers who seek assistance on their own. They are one way for the legal profession to protect the public from lawyers who breach their fiduciary duty to preserve estate or trust assets in their possession. Other remedies include monitoring programs conducted by state bar associations. Such programs, like the Texas bar program described previously in this chapter, are not yet widespread but may prove useful in helping both the offending lawyers and their victims. Another example of such an effort was evident *In re Kersey,* in which the District of Columbia Court of Appeals viewed the lawyer's alcoholism as a mitigating factor in imposing discipline and required that while the attorney was on probation he abstain from alcohol. His compliance was to be ensured by the use of a "sobriety monitor." The monitor had the authority to require the lawyer to attend Alcoholics Anonymous lawyer meetings. In addition to a sobriety monitor, the court appointed both a practice monitor to watch over professional conduct and a financial monitor who was the joint signatory with the disciplined lawyer on all client trust accounts, with access to all financial records.[18]

A great benefit of this kind of monitoring, though consuming considerable resources, is that it allows the lawyer to continue to practice. This, in turn, ensures victims a source of revenue from which to be compensated. In many of the cases detailed herein, the lawyers failed to make restitution, claiming their suspension or disbarment prevented them from earning enough money to pay back their victims.

The Lawyer Discipline Process

▼

A more general complaint about lawyers has been their insistence on self-regulation, even as they have failed in large measure to discipline their own. "Throughout history, lawyers have never vigorously enforced their rules of ethics, and this has caused serious problems. . . . And when lawyers are caught breaking the rules, severe punishment is rare."[19] State bar associations and courts typically control lawyer discipline. But many critics of the legal profession assert that "The attorney discipline system is riddled with flaws. More than 90,000 complaints are filed each year with these agencies, but only two percent of the complaints result in more than private reprimand. Clients often don't file complaints because the process takes too long, it takes place in secret, it limits clients' rights to present their own cases or to appeal decisions and it does not provide any compensation."[20] Others have argued that the lawyer discipline system is woefully underfunded across the country.[21]

According to Mary Devlin, there have been three historical phases of lawyer discipline in the United States. "The first era lasted until the end of the nineteenth century and was characterized by individual judges exercising powers necessary to control their courtrooms, not only through citing for contempt, but by striking a lawyer from the roll of attorneys. The second era of lawyer discipline began with the establishment of bar associations and advanced the law reform movement's goal of establishing unified bars. This era was characterized by volunteer attorney involvement in peer discipline. The third era is marked by a movement toward institutionalized judicial reassertion of authority over lawyer discipline with the assistance of public input."[22]

Devlin notes that toward the end of the nineteenth century, bar associations began to be formed and to focus on concerns of professionalism. The venerable Association of the Bar of the City of New

York was established in 1869 and the American Bar Association followed in 1878. Some bar associations began to investigate complaints about lawyers during this era. These associations were voluntary, and lawyers often volunteered their services to handle complaints. This system gave way to a preference for "unified" or "integrated" bar associations that handled both lawyer admissions and discipline. The perceived advantage of a unified bar was that all control over bar admission, ethics, and discipline was vested in one body and the profession policed itself. Legislatures or supreme courts performed, or set up agencies to perform, such activities in states without a unified bar. Regardless, bar associations were still not uniform in the way they approached discipline, with some reporting to their own governing boards and others reporting to the courts. Some bars appointed their own prosecutors while other states used the attorney general or other state prosecutor to bring cases against lawyers.[23]

In 1970, the ABA Special Committee on Evaluation of Disciplinary Enforcement (the "Clark Committee") characterized the American lawyer disciplinary system as "a scandalous situation that required the immediate attention of the profession. With few exceptions, the prevailing attitude of lawyers toward disciplinary enforcement ranged from apathy to outright hostility. Disciplinary action was practically nonexistent in many jurisdictions; practices and procedures [were] antiquated; [and] many disciplinary agencies had little power to take effective steps against malefactors."[24]

The Clark Committee warned the profession that public dissatisfaction was high and that the public might insist on being involved in lawyer discipline if it were not professionalized. The committee recommended that the practice of bar associations using volunteers give way to more professional procedures that included immediate suspension on the conviction of a serious crime, notice to clients of disbarred or suspended attorneys, and preventing the reinstatement of disbarred attorneys until a specified period of time had passed and the lawyer could establish that he had the necessary character to resume practice. All these things should be done "under the aegis of the jurisdiction's highest court."[25]

The ABA Standing Committee on Professional Discipline introduced the concept of public, nonlawyer members of disciplinary boards in the 1970s. In the late 1970s and 1980s, the committee also proposed Standards for Lawyer Discipline and Model Rules for Lawyer Disciplinary Enforcement. In 1989, the ABA continued its efforts with the formation of its Commission on Disciplinary Enforcement, also known as the "McKay Commission," which recommended a more expansive model of lawyer regulation, including not just disciplinary systems but "client protection or security funds; voluntary arbitration of lawyer malpractice claims and other disputes; mediation; mandatory fee arbitrations; law practice assistance; and lawyer substance abuse recovery."[26]

Devlin concludes her history of the American lawyer disciplinary process by noting that today most lawyer disciplinary bodies are under the various states' judicial branches. "The practice of law is regulated by the highest court of every state and the District of Columbia. This is in contrast to other professions and occupations which are typically regulated by agencies within the executive branch of state government. In thirty-three jurisdictions a lawyer must belong to the bar in order to practice law. In eleven unified bar jurisdictions, the lawyer disciplinary agency is separate from the bar. In the other eighteen states, an agency of the state's highest court regulates the practice of law, and lawyers pay an annual registration fee to this agency though they need not belong to the bar association in order to practice law."[27]

While lawyers may be disciplined for violating the professional rules of conduct, they are often not also prosecuted criminally for their conduct. For example, the trustees overseeing the North Carolina Bar's Client Security Fund referred to the lack of universal prosecutions of disciplined lawyers in a fall 1991 report. "Of only eight lawyers whose cases they considered in the past year, only three were tried on criminal charges and only two of the cases were for embezzlement."[28] A notable exception is the county in which Lauren Sill practiced law. In Pinellas County, Florida, State Attorney Bernie McCabe "scours Bar disciplinary reports" looking for violators to prosecute. Says McCabe, "We've insisted for several years that if the Bar comes across evidence of a crime, they better tell us about it. . . . I don't want to read about it in the Bar journal and not know anything about it."[29]

Not only the lack of prosecutions but the lack of serious sentencing, including jail time, has riled many who watch these cases of lawyer misconduct in the criminal courts. "The *[Providence] Journal Bulletin* found that punishment for the 48 lawyers who misused or stole clients' money ranged from five years in prison . . . to no criminal action at all in some cases in which lawyers made full restitution and agreed to stop practicing."[30] This discrepancy in prosecution and sentencing has been identified as one of the reasons that lawyer misconduct has increased over the years.

There is a wide disparity in disciplinary complaints among states, with one complaint for every two lawyers in upstate New York and one for every forty-two lawyers in Washington, D.C., where lawyers often work for government agencies rather than representing individuals. In arguing for abandoning the lawyer disciplinary system and relying upon the legal malpractice system to regulate lawyers, Professor Manuel Ramos of the Tulane University School of Law concludes that "The organized bar simply does not have the resources or the motivation to regulate effectively through various disciplinary proceedings."[31]

Deterrence

▼

There are a number of ways in which the legal profession could more effectively deter its members from engaging in unethical conduct. Several areas hold promise, including better enforcement of the ethical rules governing "whistleblowing" and more frequent bar discipline and criminal prosecution.

All the cases of fiduciary abuse detailed herein resulted in criminal investigation and several resulted in criminal conviction. These lawyers were either disbarred or allowed to "voluntarily resign" from their respective state bars. However, the consensus among those inside and outside of the legal profession has been that both lawyer discipline and criminal pursuit of such lawyer/fiduciaries have been inconsistent at best. When lawyers are prosecuted or disciplined, their sentences or punishments have ranged widely from probation to prison terms and from private reprimands to disbarment.[32]

There has been a call for longer and harsher sentences and disciplinary action. While this reform intuitively appeals to the public's sense of justice, it may not be the most effective way to deter lawyer/fiduciary misconduct in the future. Increasing the risk of prosecution rather than the severity of the punishment may turn out to be a much more useful tool in the effort to protect the public.

Those lawyers who get into ethical or criminal trouble are not typically risk averse. Due to their compulsions, their greed, or their desperation, they do not make "rational" evaluations about the risk of being caught. Adding jail time to those lawyers' sentences simply may be a step that is discounted by those lawyer/fiduciaries tempted to act badly. They seem to bank on the fact that they will not be caught, so longer sentences and harsher punishments make little difference in deterring them from such behavior. It may be more effective to increase the overall risk of being caught. Putting more resources into criminal prosecutions in cases of lawyer theft or in the number of bar cases disciplining egregious conflicts of interest each year may go a long way toward diluting those lawyers' tendency to think such prosecution will not happen to them.

The second problem with disbarring such lawyers and putting them in prison is the fact that it may be in large part counterproductive. As noted previously, lawyers in prison or without a ticket to practice law are unable and unlikely to pay restitution to their victims. While prison and disbarment may appeal to the public's desire to see these lawyers pay for their misconduct, it also ensures that the victims continue to suffer from the damage these lawyers have inflicted upon them.

Putting more resources into collecting judgments and monitoring lawyers allowed to go back into practice may be much more responsive to the underlying damage to the victim, though perhaps not to the reputation of the profession as a whole. It could be that these interests diverge and one must take priority over the other. The profession and the courts should focus on methods that allow such lawyers to earn a salary with the lawyering skills they have while imposing severe garnishment of wages and sale of assets to ensure restitution.

For example, a conditional license that allowed such lawyer/fiduciaries to work only under the supervision of another lawyer would allow them to earn money earmarked for restitution and would also protect the public. There are also a number of jobs lawyers do not need a license to do, for example, working in corporate positions and government agencies. The use of monitors as implemented by some state lawyer assistance programs might also be a useful tool in such cases.

A workfare program might also be an alternative to prison. Perhaps lawyer disciplinary agencies should require that such lawyers work for the overwhelmed court system or for other government agencies that require legal skills while not allowing such lawyers to take on private clients who are more vulnerable to the possibility of further attorney misconduct. In the Sill case, Florida's probate system and the victims of Sill's misconduct might have been better off with such a system. Sill's mother had been willing to exchange her own assets for a no-prison sentence for her daughter. Those assets would have benefited at least some of the victims. The court rejected the offer of "checkbook justice" for various reasons.[33] Sill's probation officer later wrote to the court that Sill was working for her mother at $670 per month, doing nonlegal work. Sill was only making $75 a month payments, which the probation officer characterized as "insufficient."[34] The court might have utilized Sill's extensive legal skills by offering to trade prison time for a workfare arrangement. She could have worked in the probate court system or for a government agency, and everyone might have been better off. Sill would probably have taken the deal to avoid prison. The court could have aggressively garnished her wages, compensating the victims much more quickly and effectively.

After all, these are economic crimes, and there should be a focus on remedies that make the victims whole, as well as punishing the offender. Creative solutions to the restitution issue might better serve the public and the profession than existing models of criminal and disciplinary sanctions.

Better funding for state lawyer assistance programs as well as for increased bar enforcement of the ethical obligation to report a fellow lawyer's serious misconduct would help deter many lawyers involved in the probate process from engaging in such misconduct in the first place. If lawyers knew that even though the court may not detect their misconduct, their colleagues were likely to report them, they might be deterred from engaging in malfeasance and misconduct. Knowing that help was available on a confidential basis might give lawyers an opportunity to pull out of the downward spiral caused by addiction. Such lawyer assistance programs and increased enforcement might also detect the problem earlier rather than later in cases where the lawyer had already embarked upon such a path.

Better funding for criminal prosecution could increase the frequency of prosecution and the consistency of sentencing. The same holds true for bar disciplinary agencies. The increased risk of being caught may have more of a deterrent effect on lawyers than would increased penalties for infrequent prosecution. Bar dues and state budgets should be increased to provide for such resources. It seems a reasonable quid pro quo for a profession that wants to continue to regulate itself.

Chapter 10

Probate in the Twenty-First Century

▼

Every civilized society needs a process to reallocate property at death. The patchwork of approaches in the United States reflects fifty different state probate codes and thousands of local probate court rules within those states. The Uniform Probate Code and its counterpart, the new Uniform Trust Code, attempt to bring uniformity and coherence to that unwieldy world. Their noninterventionist approach to probate works well, and states should continue to adopt their carefully crafted provisions. But those states must also bear in mind the need for additional resources and unilateral probate court intervention in cases where advantage may be taken of unsophisticated parties. The cases discussed in this book suggest that states must address the monitoring and information flow problems that lead to many cases of probate fraud and abuse.

Since the probate court is the venue for many cases involving Americans who are unable to protect their own interests—children, elderly, incompetents—it plays an essential role in protecting those people. The National College of Probate Judges describes this function as follows: "Probate Courts are responsible for equitably handling many kinds of problems in our society. Though they deal primarily with the estates of deceased persons, probate courts also play an important role in protecting the rights of people with special needs—the mentally ill, alcoholics, orphaned children, the aged, and developmentally disabled."[1] Given the critical function of this legal institution, states must continue to build on the reform efforts embodied in the

Uniform Probate Code and the Uniform Trust Code. Demographic, societal, and budgetary shifts must be considered on an ongoing basis in those efforts.

Back in New Hampshire

New Hampshire did initiate significant changes in its probate system in the wake of the John Fairbanks case described in Chapter 1. John Maher, past president of the National College of Probate Judges, owes his appointment as the first administrative judge of the New Hampshire probate court to the scandal.[2] Judge Maher's mandate from the New Hampshire Supreme Court was to clean up the probate system in New Hampshire. Maher viewed this daunting task as a challenge worth taking on. His appointment signaled a realization that coordination and uniformity were essential if there were to be no further Fairbanks cases in the future.

Until 1986, the New Hampshire probate structure was such that the fiduciary of an estate actually paid for the court's time to administer an estate in the form of "special session fees." Since being appointed administrative judge, Maher has overseen a variety of legislative, procedural, and structural reforms. Previously, one of the most significant flaws in the probate court process was the laissez-faire approach to the requirement that fiduciaries file accounts indicating how much money came into the estate, how much went out, and where it went. There was no computer backup and no diary of cases to keep track of them in an effective way. Years went by with little or no sanction for the failure to file accounts on the part of fiduciaries like John Fairbanks, even though by one estimate as much as one-half a billion dollars per year passes through probate in the small state of New Hampshire.

Working with the legislature, Judge Maher implemented an important innovation in probate court procedure. New legislation mandated that the probate court send out default notices if a fiduciary fails to file accounts on time. Those default notices are followed up by a citation ordering the fiduciary to show cause why he or she has failed to account. The state funded a sophisticated computer software program that produces default notices for accounts that have not been filed. The system actually requires a manual override if one wants to prevent such notices from being issued. Under Maher's supervision, the probate court staff in New Hampshire's ten counties painstakingly entered in the information on all ongoing probate court cases. It took a great deal of time and training to make sure the staff knew how to enter the data properly, but under the new system a looting of multiple estates would be detected immediately.

This legislative initiative for computerization of records was only the first of several reforms introduced. The office of the administrative judge increased the amount of judicial education about appropriate bonding policies. While the statute only required judges to bond for the amount of the taxes due on the estate, judges were encouraged to be more uniform in requiring bonds for the full amount of liquid assets in an estate. Most are now reluctant to waive the bond for such assets. Judicial education, coupled with the fear of being the judge who failed to bond an estate that was subsequently looted by a fiduciary, has resulted in more consistent bonding requirements across various county probate courts.

In addition to the computerization of records and changes in bonding policies, there have been procedural changes as well. While the legislature was initially committed to more supervision rather than less, over the ten years since the Fairbanks scandal, they have endorsed several amendments to the prevailing model of supervised administration in New Hampshire. Given the changes in recordkeeping and bonding, the state legislature felt that another case of multiple thefts was not likely to occur in New Hampshire. With that increased comfort level, they then agreed to incrementally loosen up on supervision in those cases where it seems to pose little risk to the beneficiary. Maher's role as administrative judge includes testifying before the legislature and working with it to help reform the probate statutes. In that capacity, he worked to pass legislation that essentially "waived administration" if the sole surviving beneficiary was the decedent's spouse and also the fiduciary. Such fiduciaries would not have to file a bond, an inventory, or an account because they would in essence be reporting to themselves. The following year, the legislature expanded this waiver provision to include the situation where there was no surviving spouse and an only child of the decedent was the only beneficiary and fiduciary of the decedent. This easing up on the rules provides for a more relaxed approach to the probate process and a less time-consuming and expensive process in those cases that have little risk of loss to the beneficiaries.[3]

This kind of gradual change assumes that the optimal judicial process allows for supervision but flexibility in administration. It provides for an opt-out of the probate court's supervised administration rather than the opt-in model advocated by the drafters of the Uniform Probate Code and Uniform Trust Codes. In other words, the norm is still supervised rather than unsupervised administration. Judge Maher's critique of the Uniform Probate Code in this regard is that it favors a passive role on the part of the probate court, assuming that most people will not take advantage of the vacuum in oversight left by the unsupervised model. He believes this supposition is often not borne out in the real world of the probate court. While judges and scholars can have valid disagreements about the preferred conceptual construct for American probate, all would agree that further ethical guidance and better court funding are needed to resolve the monitoring and information flow problems that continue to plague the process.

New Hampshire has continued to modernize its caseflow management, implementing timelines and a one family/one judge approach to staffing probate cases. As is typical of probate courts around the country, there is never enough money to implement all the innovations that help minimize the risk of fiduciary abuse, but Judge Maher is hopeful that the Internet and new computer applications will eventually be used to move the probate courts further in the direction of efficient case management and information flow.

The final piece of the reform puzzle is swift and consistent punishment for fiduciaries who abuse their trust. In New Hampshire, the bar is aware that such misconduct will now result in certain disbarment. The chilling effect on misconduct has had a deterrent effect on lawyer/fiduciaries contemplating fiduciary abuse.

There is also the related, and perhaps larger, problem of thefts from nonprobate, inter vivos or living trusts that are not subject to automatic probate court oversight. Beneficiaries of such trusts are ill equipped to ask the type of questions and to take the kind of action that brings probate court scrutiny to bear on living trusts. These trusts and the durable power of attorney offer people flexibility in passing their assets at death and avoiding the cumbersome and public process of guardianship. But they have resulted in some of the most egregious cases of fiduciary malfeasance and theft around the country.

Other innovations include the creative use of mediation in probate cases. Alternative dispute resolution has made its way into the legal lexicon as one of the most significant new developments in law over the past fifty years. First used in other substantive areas of law, it has now come to probate. In New Hampshire, mediators help resolve issues that would otherwise end up in litigation, using up the probate court's limited resources and the estate's assets in litigation fees. This in turn helps relieve an already overburdened judiciary. It also improves the average citizen's view of the process if a greater number of people can achieve a result with less acrimony than that engendered by litigation.

While there is still the opportunity for a single theft by a single fiduciary in the New Hampshire probate process, the reforms introduced since the Fairbanks scandal have minimized the chances that a similar widespread looting of estates could occur again in that state.[4] California, New York, Virginia, and Florida have also adopted individual reforms in the wake of their respective scandals, but New Hampshire has adopted the most comprehensive reforms. Whether the New Hampshire model could be effective in other, larger states waits to be seen.

The first years of the twenty-first century have brought significant change to the American system of transferring property at death. We have seen Congress phase out the federal estate tax and the National Conference of Commissioners on Uniform State Laws introduce a comprehensive new Uniform Trust Code. The nation's banks are consolidating, eliminating the option of institutional fiduciary services for many middle-class Americans, and Americans continue to live longer, a fact that increases the need for more fiduciaries like guardians and trustees. All of these changes implicate the fifty state probate court systems. Changes to the federal estate tax mean changes to the state inheritance and estate taxes and changes in some state court procedures. The adoption of the new Uniform Trust Code by states will affect probate courts. The lack of institutional trustees and the need for more guardians will force probate courts to respond. Internet access also offers the new possibility of increased supervision with greater efficiency, if states fully fund court budgets. Probate also exists in the larger world of the American legal system. Recent trends in the broader profession, like the movement toward multidisciplinary practice (removing the ethical barriers to lawyers practicing with nonlawyers) and alternative dispute resolution, will affect the probate process as well.

The desire to pass on one's legacy in the form of an inheritance is a universal desire. It is among the most fundamental of human concerns, and the issue of how best to reallocate property at death has engaged the law since the advent of individual ownership of property. American probate courts provide the vehicle for an orderly post-death disposition of property that balances the interests of creditors, the government and the heirs and beneficiaries of the deceased. It also plays a protective role in the lives of many of America's most vulnerable citizens. In working to further reform probate, America's legal profession and its judiciary are engaged in a noble pursuit that embodies Justice Felix Frankfurter's description of lawyers when he wrote that "[they act] in defense of right and to ward off wrong."[5] Those words should continue to guide the legal profession into the twenty-first century.

Notes

▼

Preface

1. Adam Nagourney, "A Nation Challenged: Estate Planning: Jolted by Sept. 11, Many Rush to Make Wills," New York Times, 13 December 2001.

Chapter 1
The Purposes of Probate

1. Pat Grossmith, "Fairbanks Ends Life on Run. Questions Remain for Fugitive's Sister, Other Victims," *Manchester Union Leader,* 29 March 1994.
2. New Hampshire House of Representatives, Report of the First House Committee to Study the State Investigation of the John C. Fairbanks Matter, Part IV, Concord, N.H., (hereafter cited as First Committee Report), 1997, 1.
3. First Committee Report, Part IV, 1.
4. Brad Hills, "Insurance Company Agrees to Settle Estate Bond Involving Fugitive Judge," *Manchester Union Leader,* 2 August 1990.
5. First Committee Report, Part IV, 1.
6. Ibid.
7. Ibid.
8. New Hampshire Constitution, art. 71.
9. First Committee Report, Part IV, 2.
10. *Meding v. Fleet Bank*, No. 91-E-029, (Sullivan County N.H. Superior Court), Order of 22 July 1993, 2–3.
11. Ibid., 3.
12. Ibid.
13. Ibid., 4.
14. Ibid.
15. Ibid., 5–6.
16. Ibid., 6.
17. Ibid., 1, 6.
18. Ibid., 13.
19. First Committee Report, Part IV, 2.
20. Ibid.
21. Ibid.
22. Ibid., 4.
23. Ibid.
24. Ibid.
25. Ibid., 5.
26. Ibid., 3.
27. Ibid.
28. Ibid.
29. Ibid.
30. Hills, "Insurance Company Agrees To Settle"; First Committee Report, Part IV, 5.
31. First Committee Report, Part IV, 5.
32. Ibid., 5.
33. Ibid.
34. Roger Talbot, "Chief: Fairbanks Dozed in Court, Heard Cases in Privacy," *Manchester Union Leader,* 1 October 1997.
35. New Hampshire Almanac, "A Brief History of New Hampshire" (retrieved from www.state.nh.us/nhinfo/history.html).
36. National College of Probate Judges, Web site (www.ncpj.org).
37. *Webster's New International Dictionary*, 3d ed., 1961, cited in John F. Winkler, "The Probate Courts of Ohio," *University of Toledo Law Review* 28 (1997): 563, 566 n. 23.
38. Jesse Dukeminier and Stanley M. Jo-

hanson, *Wills, Trusts, and Estates*, 5th ed. (Boston: Little, Brown, 1995), 38.
39. Ibid., 38–39.
40. Thomas E. Atkinson, "The Development of the Massachusetts Probate System," *Michigan Law Review* 42 (1943): 425–26.
41. For an interesting analysis of the variety of approaches to probate jurisdiction in the United States, see Lewis Simes and Paul E. Basye, "The Organization of the Probate Court in America," *Michigan Law Review* 42 (1944): 965.
42. First Committee Report, Part VI, 2.
43. Commission on National Probate Court Standards and Advisory Committee on Interstate Guardianships, *National Probate Court Standards* (1993), 1.
44. Ibid., 4.
45. Ibid., 4–5.
46. Ibid., 5–6.
47. Ibid., 6.
48. For a succinct summary of probate procedure and the purposes of probate, see Dukeminier and Johanson, *Wills, Trusts, and Estates*, 41.
49. Ibid., 37–38.
50. Ibid.
51. Ibid., 1–2.
52. Ibid., 1.
53. Ibid., 2.
54. First Committee Report, Part IV, 5.
55. Ibid., 6.
56. Ibid.
57. Ibid., 6–7.
58. Ibid., 7.
59. Michael Cousineau, "Judge Finds Fleet Liable," *Manchester Union Leader*, 23 July 1993.
60. Grossmith, "Fairbanks Ends Life on the Run."
61. Ibid.
62. Cousineau, "Judge Finds Fleet Liable."
63. Grossmith, "Fairbanks Ends Life on the Run."
64. Ibid.
65. First Committee Report, Part IV, 7.
66. Ibid.
67. New Hampshire Laws, Chapter 254, "An Act Establishing A House Committee to Study the State Investigation of the Late John D. Fairbanks" (HB 1593-FN 1996).
68. First Committee Report, Part III, "Statement of Purpose."
69. Ibid., Part V, 4–5.
70. Ibid., 5, citing Transcript of Meeting of September 18, 1996, 40.
71. Ibid., 7, citing Transcript of Meeting of October 2, 1996, 30.
72. Roger Talbot, "Fairbanks, Round II: Questions Remain," *Manchester Union Leader*, 4 January 1998.
73. First Committee Report, Part V, 10, citing Transcript of Meeting of 30 October 1996, 22.
74. Ibid., Summary of Meeting of 30 October 1996.
75. Ibid., 12, Summary of Meeting of 6 November 1996.
76. Ibid., 12–13, Summary of Meeting of 6 November 1996.
77. Ibid., 13, Summary of Meeting of 12 November 1996.
78. Ibid., 14, Summary of Meeting of 12 November 1996.
79. First Committee Report, Part VI, 1.
80. Ibid.
81. Ibid.
82. Ibid., 2.
83. Ibid.
84. Ibid., 2–3.
85. First Committee Report, Part VII, 1.
86. Roger Talbot, "Fairbanks Report Now Available for Public Inspection," *Manchester Union Leader*, 25 January 1997.
87. Meeting of Second Committee to Study the Investigation of John C. Fairbanks and others, New Hampshire Legislature, (Concord, 30 October 1997), Author's Notes.
88. Talbot, "Fairbanks Report Now Available."
89. Talbot, "Fairbanks, Round II."
90. Ibid.
91. Ralph Jimenez, "Controversy Engulfs Court, Allegations against Jurist Add to Atmosphere of Suspicion," *Boston Globe*, 3 October 1999.
92. Katherine Webster, "Judges Struggle to Keep Their Independence in Face of Court Reform," Associated Press, 22 March 1999.

Chapter 2
Lawyers as Fiduciaries

1. Joe Calderone and Kevin McCoy, "Cuomo Trusted Him, Too," *Newsday*, 15 February 1992.

2. Kevin McCoy, "Tearful Biegen Says He's Sorry; Gets 2nd Sentence in $1M Theft," *Newsday*, 5 November 1992.
3. In the Matter of Arnold Biegen, 582 NYS2d 157, 158 (1992).
4. Ralph Blumenthal, "Former Dinkins Aide Pleads Guilty to Two Charges of Theft," *New York Times*, 12 February 1992.
5. Ibid.
6. Kevin McCoy and Joe Calderone, "For Victim of Biegen, Anger Is All That Is Left," *Newsday*, 13 February 1992.
7. Blumenthal, "Former Dinkins Aide Pleads Guilty."
8. McCoy and Calderone, "For Victim of Biegen."
9. Ibid.
10. Calderone and McCoy, "Cuomo Trusted Him."
11. Blumenthal, "Former Dinkins Aide Pleads Guilty."
12. Joe Calderone and Kevin McCoy, "Biegen Cuts a Deal; Pleads Guilty, Talks to Prosecutors," *Newsday*, 28 May 1992.
13. Blumenthal, "Former Dinkins Aide Pleads Guilty."
14. Ibid.
15. Gary Spencer, "Parker Chapin Could Be Liable Due to Biegen; Question of Supervision Raised by Conservator," *New York Law Journal*, 19 February 1992.
16. Blumenthal, "Former Dinkins Aide Pleads Guilty."
17. Ibid.
18. Spencer, "Parker Chapin Could Be Liable."
19. Ibid.
20. *Clients' Security Fund v. Grandeau*, 72 NY2d 62 (1988).
21. Spencer, "Parker Chapin Could Be Liable."
22. Ibid.
23. Calderone and McCoy, "Cuomo Trusted Him."
24. Ronald Sullivan, "Prison Term Completes Political Fall From Grace," *New York Times*, 30 October 1992.
25. Calderone and McCoy, "Biegen Cuts a Deal."
26. Joe Calderone and Kevin McCoy, "Biegen Disbarred Two Months after Admitting Thefts," *Newsday*, 8 April 1992.
27. In the Matter of Arnold Biegen, 158.
28. Joe Calderone, "Mayor Got Free Ride, Firm Paid for Car Service," *Newsday*, 7 October 1992.
29. Ronald Sullivan, "Prison Term Completes Fall."
30. Ronald Sullivan, "Dinkins' Former Aide Is Sentenced for Embezzlement," *New York Times*, 5 November 1992.
31. Calderone and McCoy, "Biegen Cuts a Deal."
32. Kevin McCoy, "Biegen Used Cop's Social Security Number," *Newsday*, 23 February 1992.
33. Sullivan, "Prison Term Completes Fall."
34. Kevin McCoy, "Biegen Scandal Coming to End." Newsday, 29 October 1992.
35. *Black's Law Dictionary*, 5th ed. (St. Paul: West, 1979), 563. For a more detailed discussion of many of the ideas in this chapter, see Paula A. Monopoli, "Fiduciary Duty: A New Ethical Paradigm for Lawyer/Fiduciaries," *Missouri Law Review* 67 (2002): 309.
36. Black's Law Dictionary.
37. Edward D. Spurgeon and Mary Jane Ciccarello, "The Lawyer in Other Fiduciary Roles: Policy and Ethical Considerations," *Fordham Law Review* 62 (1994): 1359.
38. Spurgeon and Ciccarello, "The Lawyer in Other Fiduciary Roles," 1376. As Spurgeon and Ciccarello note, the 1908 Canons of Professional Responsibility, the precursor to the 1969 Model Code, was interpreted to prohibit the practice of lawyers acting as executors. Spurgeon and Ciccarello cite Henry S. Drinker, *Legal Ethics* (New York: Columbia University Press, 1953), 94, and Joseph A. deFuria Jr., "A Matter of Ethics Ignored: The Attorney-Draftsman as Testamentary Fiduciary," *Kansas Law Review* 36 (1988): 277. Both Drinker and deFuria note the profession's apparent lack of attention in the literature and case law with lawyer/fiduciaries. See Spurgeon and Ciccarello, "The Lawyer in Other Fiduciary Roles," 1375–76, n. 73–74.
39. "The American Bar Association Model Code of Professional Responsibility Ethical Consideration 5–6," in *Professional Responsibility Standards Rules & Statutes*, 1998–99, ed. John S. Dzien-

kowski (St. Paul: West Group, 1998), 429.

40. Spurgeon and Ciccarello, "The Lawyer in Other Fiduciary Roles," 1376.
41. "The American Bar Association Model Rules of Professional Conduct Rule 1.8, Legal Background" (Proposed Final Draft 1981), cited in Spurgeon and Ciccarello, "The Lawyer in Other Fiduciary Roles," 1377.
42. American College of Trust & Estate Counsel (ACTEC), "Comment on Rule 1.7," in *Commentaries to the Model Rules of Professional Conduct* (Los Angeles: ACTEC, 1993), 91.
43. American Bar Association, ABA Ethics 2000 Commission on the Evaluation of the Rules of Professional Conduct, final report, Chicago, 2000, Rule 1.8(c) cmt. 8.
44. ACTEC, "Comment on Rule 1.7," 91. The ACTEC commentary to Rule 1.7 also notes in the paragraph entitled "Selection of Fiduciaries" that "The lawyer advising a client regarding the selection and appointment of a fiduciary should make full disclosure to the client of any benefits that the lawyer may receive as a result of the appointment. In particular, the lawyer should inform the client of any policies or practices known to the lawyer that the fiduciaries under consideration may follow with respect to the employment of the scrivener of an estate planning document as counsel for the fiduciary. The lawyer may also point out that a fiduciary has the right to choose any counsel it wishes."
45. Louis D. Laurino, "The Duties and Responsibilities of the Attorney/Fiduciary," Annual Lecture at the University of Miami Philip E. Heckerling Inst. On Est. Plan. 19 (John T. Gaubatz ed. 1985): ¶ 1601.2 describing a 1975 American Bar Foundation comparative study of estate administration in the United States.
46. Spurgeon and Ciccarello, "The Lawyer in Other Fiduciary Roles," 1357.
47. Spurgeon and Ciccarello, "The Lawyer in Other Fiduciary Roles," 1384, citing ABA Section of Real Property, Probate & Trust Law, "Principles for Attorneys Acting in Other Fiduciary Roles," Chicago, 16 October 1992. In an article seeking comments on the proposed principles, Bradley R. Cook states that while the Section Council of the American Bar Association Real Property, Probate and Trust Law Section believes that it is appropriate for a drafting attorney to act as an executor or trustee, "performing in such roles carries additional responsibilities and certain risks for the attorney, no attorney should undertake to serve as an executor, trustee or other fiduciary without being properly trained and equipped to perform all of the associated tasks in a competent and efficient manner." Bradley R. Cook, "Principles for Attorneys Acting in Other Fiduciary Roles," *Probate & Property* (March/April 1992): 6. See also the recent American Bar Association Committee on Ethics and Professional Responsibility Formal Opinion 02–426 *Lawyer Serving as Fiduciary for an Estate or Trust,* 31 May 2002.
48. ABA Section of Real Property, Probate & Trust Law, "Principles for Attorneys": Principle 9.
49. Spurgeon and Ciccarello, "The Lawyer in Other Fiduciary Roles," 1368 n. 47, cite several articles in which "some commentators have also pointed out that for business reasons, lawyers should accept opportunities to be a fiduciary, as the changing nature of estate planning law is curtailing the amount of legal work needed in the field."
50. Jeffrey N. Pennell, "Ethics, Professionalism, and Malpractice Issues in Estate Planning and Administration," *American Law Institute–American Bar Association Course of Study* 75 (1988): 168.
51. Ibid., 166.
52. Joshua S. Rubenstein, "Compensation of Attorney/Executors: Practitioners often Caught Between Scylla and Charybdis," *New York Law Journal*, 29 April 1996.

Chapter 3
Probate Avoidance

1. Davan Maharaj, "Leisure World Lawyer Heir to Clients' Millions," *Los Angeles Times*, 22 November 1992.

2. John H. Westover, Esq., Counsel for Plaintiffs/Respondents in Estate of Merrill A. Miller, telephone interview, 29 October 1999.
3. Ibid.
4. Ibid.
5. Estate of Merrill A. Miller, Deceased unpublished opinion; *Mary McWethy et al. v. James D. Gunderson*, 4th App. Dist., Division Three no. G016789 consolidated with G017879 (April 22, 1998), Orange County Superior Court no. A-166214, respondents' brief, 22 citing Harold Stromsen deposition, 32–33.
6. Estate of Merrill A. Miller, unpublished opinion, 2.
7. Ibid.
8. Ibid.
9. Estate of Merrill A. Miller, respondents' brief, 7 n. 3 citing R.T., pp. 317–18, Exhibit 12.
10. Estate of Merrill A. Miller, unpublished opinion, 2–3.
11. Estate of Merrill A. Miller, respondents' brief, 26 citing R.T. Vol. III, pp. 117–21.
12. Ibid., 31.
13. Estate of Merrill A. Miller, unpublished opinion, 3.
14. Ibid., 2–3.
15. Estate of Merrill A. Miller, respondents' brief, 32.
16. Estate of Merrill A. Miller, Unpublished Opinion, 3–4.
17. *Magee v. State Bar of California*, 58 Cal2d 423 (1962), 431.
18. American Bar Association, Model Rules of Professional Conduct as amended February 2002, (Chicago: American Bar Association, 2002), Rule 1.8(c).
19. Rules of Professional Conduct of the State Bar of California, Rule 4–400 (2001).
20. Rule 4–400, Drafter's Notes (1988) citing *Magee v. State Bar.*
21. Estate of Merrill A. Miller, unpublished opinion, 8.
22. Maharaj, "Leisure World Lawyer Heir."
23. Davan Maharaj, "O. C. Attorney Quits the Law," *Los Angeles Times*, 11 January 1994.
24. Estate of Merrill A. Miller, respondents' brief, 8–9.
25. Davan Maharaj, "Judge Removes O. C. Lawyer as Estates' Trustee," *Los Angeles Times*, 12 December 1992.
26. Davan Maharaj, "Lawyer Defends Bequest to Him by Client," *Los Angeles Times*, 20 May 1994.
27. Estate of Merrill A. Miller, respondents' brief, 21 citing R.T. Vol. IX, pp. 2422, 1143, 1304, 1315, 1324–25, 1262–72, 1302–5, 1266, 1143, 1287, 1296–97, 1294–97.
28. Ibid., 21–22 citing R.T. Vol. IV, pp. 179–80; Exhibit 100, p. Bates no. S0013; and R.T. Vol. XIII, pp. 1949–50.
29. Ibid., 22–23 citing R.T. Vol. VI pp. 586–587; deposition of Stromsen offered in evidence at Vol. V, p. 375, Depo., pp. 32–33, 14–15; and R.T. Vol. IX, pp. 1148–49.
30. Jonathan Volzke, "Former Attorney's 38-Year Career Under Fire," *Orange County Register,* 19 June 1994.
31. Lynn Franey, "Doctor Doubts Mental Ability of Man Who Left Gunderson Money," *Los Angeles Times*, Orange County Edition, 21 May 1994.
32. Estate of Merrill A. Miller, unpublished opinion, 4–5.
33. Ibid., 8.
34. See the cases described in Estate of Merrill A. Miller, respondents' brief, 8–19.
35. Ibid., 7 n. 3.
36. Tully H. Seymour, "Living Trusts, Probate Court Duties in Safeguarding Estates Reviewed," letter, *Los Angeles Times*, 20 December 1993.
37. Norman F. Dacey, *How to Avoid Probate—Updated!* (New York: Crown, 1980), 15.
38. Jesse Dukeminier and Stanley M. Johanson, *Wills, Trusts, and Estates*, 5th ed. (Boston: Little, Brown, 1995), 47.
39. John H. Langbein, "The Nonprobate Revolution and the Future of the Law of Succession," *Harvard Law Review* 97 (1984): 1117.
40. Ibid., 1118–19.
41. Note that life insurance companies and retirement fund trustees are corporate bureaucracies, with, arguably, little incentive to misdirect or steal the assets. However, many living trust trustees are family members, vulnerable to mistakes or intentional misbe-

havior in distributing trust assets. When individual lawyers are trustees, they also face conflicts of interest and the temptation to divert trust assets to their own benefit.

42. Langbein, 1120–22.
43. Ibid., 1118 n. 45.
44. Ibid., 1128–29.
45. Ibid., 1139–1140.
46. Ibid., 1116 citing Richard V. Wellman, "The Uniform Probate Code, A Possible Answer to Probate Avoidance," *Indiana Law Journal* 44 (1969): 191, 193, 1117.
47. Estate of Merrill A. Miller, unpublished opinion, 3.
48. Merrill A. Miller Trust (Minute Order; Orange County, California Superior Court No. A-166214, entered 17 August 1994).
49. Westover, telephone interview; see also the cases described in Estate of Merrill A. Miller, respondents' brief, 8–19.
50. Seymour, "Living Trusts."
51. Ibid.
52. Maharaj, "Leisure World Lawyer Heir."
53. Davan Maharaj, "O. C. Lawyer's Estate Cases Probed by Bar," *Los Angeles Times*, 25 November 1992. See also Davan Maharaj, "Hot Line Seeks 'Victimized' Clients of Lawyer," *Los Angeles Times*, 2 December 1992.
54. Maharaj, "O. C. Lawyer's Estate Cases Probed."
55. Maharaj, "Judge Removes O. C. Lawyer."
56. Maharaj, "Leisure World Lawyer Heir."
57. Maharaj, "Judge Removes O. C. Lawyer."
58. Westover, telephone interview.
59. Dan Weikel and Davan Maharaj, "Bar to Review Rules on Estate Gifts to Lawyers," *Los Angeles Times*, 27 December 1992.
60. Ibid.
61. ABA Ethics 2000, Final Report, Rule 1.8(c) cmt. 8.
62. Eric Bailey and Davan Maharaj, "Bill to Safeguard Estates from Lawyers Gains," *Los Angeles Times*, 11 February 1993.
63. Eric Bailey and Davan Maharaj, "Assembly Oks Bill to Ban Client Bequests to Lawyers," *Los Angeles Times*, Orange County Edition, 17 July 1993. See also Eric Bailey and Davan Maharaj, "New Law to Curb Will-Drafting Abuses," *Los Angeles Times*, 3 August 1993.
64. Bailey and Maharaj, "Assembly Oks Bill"; see also Bailey and Maharaj, "New Law to Curb Will-Drafting Abuses."
65. Maharaj, "O. C. Attorney Gunderson Quits."
66. "A Lawyer Just One Step Ahead of the Law," editorial, *Los Angeles Times*, Orange County Edition, 30 January 1994.

Chapter 4
Complexity and Corruption

1. John H. Langbein, "Undue Influence: The Epic Battle for the Johnson & Johnson Fortune (Book Review)," *Yale Law Journal* 103 (1994): 2039, 2045 n. 17 citing Jesse Dukeminier and Stanley M. Johanson, *Wills, Trusts, and Estates*, 4th ed. (Boston: Little, Brown, 1990), 33 n.10 quoting Goldstein, "Once More, Surrogate Talks," *New York Times*, 4 September 1977.
2. John H. Langbein, "The Nonprobate Revolution and the Future of the Law of Succession," *Harvard Law Review* 97 (1984): 1108, 1117.
3. Norman F. Dacey, *How to Avoid Probate—Updated!* (New York: Crown, 1980), 17.
4. Ibid., 21.
5. See Robert A. Stein and Ian G. Fierstein, "The Demography of Probate Administration," *University of Baltimore Law Review* 15 (1985): 54, which cites a study in five states showing that between 20 and 34 percent of the estates of adults who died in those states were actually administered.
6. See Lawrence H. Averill Jr., "An Eclectic History and Analysis of the 1990 Uniform Probate Code," *Albany Law Review* 55 (1992): 891, 896.
7. Uniform Probate Code, Uniform Laws Annotated (St. Paul: West, 1999), Part I, 1.
8. Uniform Probate Code, General Comment, Article III, 26, 28.

9. Uniform Probate Code, sec. 3–501, 105.
10. Uniform Probate Code, General Comment, Article III, 26, 28.
11. Richard V. Wellman, "Georgia Lawyers Revise Their Code," *Georgia State University Law Review* 13 (1997): 783.
12. Uniform Probate Code, sec. 3–501, 105.
13. Ibid., sec. 3–504, 108.
14. Ibid., sec. 3–603, 115.
15. Ibid., sec. 3–1001, 288.
16. Uniform Probate Code, General Comment, Article VII, 486.
17. California Probate Code, sec. 15642 (St. Paul: West, 1998).

Chapter 5
Delays and Deception

1. Nicholas Riccardi and Greg Krikorian, "State's Child Support Computer Plan Rejected," *Los Angeles Times*, 10 April 1999.
2. Ronald Smothers, "Virgin Mary Seen in State Paperwork," *New York Times*, 7 January 2000.
3. Virginia State Bar, Special Committee on Lawyers Serving as Fiduciaries, Report to the Council of the Virginia State Bar, Recommendations in Favor of a Program of Random Reviews, (Richmond, 1993), 11.
4. Ibid., 12.
5. Jill Schachner Chanen, "Keeping a Lid on Illegal Takings: Commonsense Procedures Can Keep Employees' Hands Out of the Cookie Jar," *ABA Journal* 85 (June 1999): 74–75.
6. Witness affidavit of David Kurash, Investigator with State Attorney's Office, Sixth Judicial Circuit of Florida, *State of Florida v. Lauren Ann Sill*, Case #93-05819CFANO, Criminal Court File (Circuit Court, Pinellas County).
7. Chanen, "Keeping a Lid on Illegal Takings."
8. *New York County Lawyers' Association v. Dacey*, 282 NYS2d 985 (1967).
9. See Justice Stevens' dissent in ibid.
10. Debra Baker, "Is This Woman a Threat to Lawyers?" *ABA Journal* 85 (June 1999): 54–55.
11. *The Supreme Court of Texas Unauthorized Practice of Law Committee v. Nolo Press Inc.* UPLC File: HOU-97-067 (1997). The investigation was dismissed in a Letter to Pete Kennedy, Esq., George & Donaldson, L.L.P., counsel for Nolo Press, September 21, 1999. For a detailed description of the UPLC's actions in the case see Brief on the Merits of Relator Nolo Press, Statement of Facts, In the Supreme Court of Texas, In Re Nolo Press/Folk Law Inc., filed September 8, 1998 (available at www.nolo.com/Texas/Merits-Nolo.html).
12. Pete Kennedy, counsel for Nolo Press, telephone interview, 24 March 2000.
13. Ibid.
14. Ibid.
15. Ibid.
16. The bill was HB 1507 that amended Section 81.101 of the Texas Statutes defining the practice of law. That amendment, by Acts 1999, 76th Leg., ch. 799, s. 1, effective June 18, 1999 provided that the "practice of law" "does not include the design, creation, publication, distribution, display or sale, including publication, distribution, display, or sale by means of an Internet web site, of written materials, books, forms, computer software, or similar products if the products clearly and conspicuously state that the products are not a substitute for the advice of an attorney."
17. Kennedy, telephone interview.
18. Baker, "Is This Woman a Threat," citing Judge Barefoot Sanders' opinion in *Unauthorized Practice of Law Committee v. Parsons Technology, Inc. d/b/a Quicken Family Lawyer* (No. Civ.A. 3:97CV-2859H) 1999 WL 47235 (N.D. Tex.).
19. *Unauthorized Practice of Law Committee v. Parsons Technology, Inc. d/b/a Quicken Family Lawyer,* 179 F3d 956 (1999).
20. www.halt.org/FLIP/fliphome.html.
21. James Podgers, "Confidence Game: Bench, Bar Leaders Ponder Strategies to Raise Public Trust in the Courts," *ABA Journal* 85 (July 1999): 86.
22. Philip S. Anderson, "Learning to Educate the Public," *ABA Journal* 85 (July 1999): 6.
23. Leland Alan Stark, *How to Live—and Die—with California Probate: Wills,*

Trusts, and Estate Planning in Layman's Language, 3d ed. (Gulf Publishing, 1991).

24. Judge Mary Sheffield, Past President, National College of Probate Court Judges, interview with author, Baltimore, Md., 31 March 2000.
25. Judge John Maher, President, National College of Probate Court Judges, interview with author, Baltimore, Md., 31 March 2000.
26. Baker, "Is This Woman a Threat."

Chapter 6
Meager Judicial Resources

1. *State of Florida v. Lauren Ann Sill*, Case #93-05819CFANO, (Criminal Court File Circuit Court, Pinellas County), witness affidavit of David A. Kurash, Investigator with State Attorney's Office, Sixth Judicial Circuit of Florida, 21 April 1993.
2. *State of Florida v. Lauren Ann Sill*, Sentencing Memorandum (Statement of Facts) 31 January 1994, 1–2.
3. This is the compelling account of the courtroom exchange as described by Jeffrey Good in his Pulitzer Prize-winning editorial investigation "Final Indignities"; Good, "Broken Promises, Perspective," *St. Petersburg Times*, 28 August 1994.
4. Jeffrey Good, "A Sorry Chapter in Local Legal History," *St. Petersburg Times*, 19 December 1993.
5. Ibid.
6. Order dated 4 February 1993, *The Florida Bar v. Lauren A. Sill*, (Florida Supreme Court Case No. 80,115).
7. This account of the case was taken from a letter of Eva R. Joline, 6 January 1994, *State of Florida v. Lauren Ann Sill*, filed with the court prior to Lauren Sill's sentencing.
8. Ibid.
9. Ibid.
10. *The Florida Bar v. Lauren A. Sill*, order dated 4 February 1993.
11. *State of Florida v. Lauren Ann Sill*, letter of Eva R. Joline.
12. Stephen Nohlgren, "Guardian Lawyer Is Suspended over Trust Fund," *St. Petersburg Times*, 5 February 1993.
13. *State of Florida v. Lauren Ann Sill*, letter of Shirley Pence, 31 January 1994.
14. *State of Florida v. Lauren Ann Sill*, letter of Charlene T. Romanello, 15 January 1994.
15. *State of Florida v. Lauren Ann Sill*, witness affidavit of David A. Kurash, 3–4.
16. Ibid., 1–2.
17. *State of Florida v. Lauren Ann Sill*, letter from Pedro J. Pizarro, C.P.A. to Joseph A. Corsmeir, Esq. Assistant Staff Counsel, The Florida Bar, 1, Appendix to witness affidavit of David A. Kurash.
18. Ibid.
19. Ibid., 2.
20. *The Florida Bar v. Lauren A. Sill*, 620 So.2d 763, 26 April 1993 (Florida Supreme Court Case No. 81,628); *The Florida Bar v. Lauren A. Sill*, 630 So.2d 1102, 9 December 1993 (Case No. 82,437).
21. *State of Florida v. Lauren Ann Sill*, witness affidavit of David A. Kurash, 3–5, quote at 5.
22. *State of Florida v. Lauren Ann Sill*, Sentencing Memorandum (Statement of Facts), 2.
23. Ibid., 2–4.
24. *State of Florida v. Lauren Ann Sill*, Change of Plea Form, 16 December 1993.
25. For prosecutor's recommended sentence, see *State of Florida v. Lauren Ann Sill*, Sentencing Memorandum (Statement of Facts) at 6–11.
26. *State of Florida v. Lauren Ann Sill*, Reconsideration of Sentence, 23 March 1994, 4–8.
27. Ibid., 14–15.
28. Jeffrey Good, "She Paid for Her Crimes—Didn't She?" *St. Petersburg Times*, City Edition 26 March 1995.
29. Ibid.
30. *State of Florida v. Lauren Ann Sill*, letter of Nancy Josa, 11 January 1994.
31. *State of Florida v. Lauren Ann Sill*, letter of Eva Joline.
32. John H. Langbein, "Will Contests," book review, *Yale Law Journal* 103 (1994): 2039, 2044.
33. Ibid., 2044.
34. Ibid., 2045.
35. Winnie Hu, "Favoritism by Judges Faces Study," *New York Times*, 11 January 2000.
36. "The Cozy World of Judges and Law-

yers," editorial, *New York Times*, 15 January 2000.
37. Elise Ackerman, "You Can't Take It with You," *Miami New Times*, 28 March 1996.
38. Ibid.
39. Ibid.
40. National College of Probate Judges Web site, www.ncpj.org.
41. Ibid.
42. Ibid., activities (www.ncpj.org).
43. Ibid., goals (www.ncpj.org).
44. A. Frank Johns, speech to the National College of Probate Judges, Spring Seminar, Baltimore, Md., 31 March 2000, Author's Notes.
45. Commission on National Probate Court Standards and Advisory Committee on Interstate Guardianships, *National Probate Court Standards* (1993), 2.
46. Ibid., 2–3.
47. Ibid., Standard 2.2 "Caseflow Management," 31.
48. Ibid., Standard 2.2.1 "Court Control," 31 n. 14 quoting American Bar Association Division for Judicial Services and Lawyers Conference Task Force on Reduction of Litigation Cost and Delay, "Defeating Delay" report, Chicago, 1986, 24.
49. Ibid., Standard 2.2.1 "Court Control" and Standard 2.2.2 "Court Supervision of Case Progress," 31–32.
50. Ibid., Commentary to Standard 2.2.3 "Time Standards Governing Disposition," 33; Commentary to Standard 2.2.1 "Court Control," 32.
51. Ibid., Commentary to Standard 2.2.3, "Time Standards Governing Disposition," 33–34.
52. Ibid., Appendix B, 118.
53. Dan Weikel and Davan Maharaj, "Bar to Review Rules on Estate Gifts to Lawyers," *Los Angeles Times*, Orange County Edition, 27 December 1992.
54. *National Probate Court Standards*, Standard 2.3.2, 36.
55. Donna Hunzeker, "Legislative-Judicial Relations: Seeking a New Partnership," National Conference of State Legislatures, 1 July 1990.
56. Pamela Martineau, "George Urges Lawmakers to Stabilize Court Funding, Speed Capital Appeals," *Metropolitan News-Enterprise*, 16 May 1996.
57. Matthew T. Crosson, "Third Branch of Government Deserves Fair Share of Budget," *New York Law Journal*, 27 January 1993.
58. Ibid.
59. Karen Maeshiro, "Judge Tours A.V. Court: State's Chief Justice Calls Crowding Worst He's Seen," *Daily News of Los Angeles*, 14 April 1998.

Chapter 7
A Conspiracy of Silence

1. Howard Gleckman and Ann Therese Palmer, "States: A Rebound Won't End Red Ink," *BusinessWeek*, 17 June 2002, 60–61.
2. Jeffrey Good, "A Sorry Chapter in Local Legal History," *St. Petersburg Times*, 19 December 1993.
3. Jeffrey Good, "Broken Promises, Final Indignities: An Investigation" *St. Petersburg Times*, 28 August 1994.
4. "The American Bar Association Model Code of Professional Responsibility," DR 1–103(A), in John S. Dzienkowski, ed., *Professional Responsibility Standards Rules & Statues*, 1998–99 ed. (St. Paul: West Group, 1998), 389.
5. The American Bar Association Model Rules of Professional Conduct, as amended February 2002, (Chicago: American Bar Association, 2002) Rule 8.3(a).
6. Ken Armstrong, "Lawyers Go after Own—Bar None," *Chicago Tribune*, 30 December 1996.
7. *In re Himmel*, 125 Ill2d 531 (1988), 535.
8. Ibid.
9. Ibid., 535–36.
10. Ibid., 536–37.
11. Ibid., 536–39.
12. Ibid., 534–35, 546.
13. Armstrong, "Lawyers Go After Own."
14. Ibid.
15. "Should Attorneys Have an Obligation to Report Disciplinary Violations of Others?" *Massachusetts Lawyers Weekly*, 5 August 1996.
16. Ibid.
17. Russell G. Pearce, "Teaching Ethics Seriously: Legal Ethics as the Most Important Subject in Law School," *Loyola University of Chicago Law Journal* 29 (Summer 1998): 719.

18. Pearce, "Teaching Ethics Seriously," 722, quoting Deborah L. Rhode, "Ethics by the Pervasive Method," *Journal of Legal Education* 42 (1992): 31, 35, 37.
19. Pearce, "Teaching Ethics Seriously," 723, 724.
20. Pearce, "Teaching Ethics Seriously," 726, 728.
21. Michael Millemann, "The Institutional Barriers and Advantages Panel," *William and Mary Law Review* 39 (1998): 489, 506 n. 23.
22. Manuel R. Ramos, "Legal and Law School Malpractice: Confessions of a Lawyer's Lawyer and Law Professor," *Ohio State Law Journal* 57 (1996): 863, 882.
23. Pearce, "Teaching Ethics Seriously," 733, quoting John Mixon and Robert P. Schuwerk, "The Personal Dimension of Professional Responsibility," *Law and Contemporary Problems*, Summer–Autumn 1995, 87, 98.
24. Pearce, "Teaching Ethics Seriously," 735, quoting Deborah L. Rhode, "Ethics by the Pervasive Method," 46–47.
25. Ibid., 48.
26. Jeffrey Pennell, "Ethics, Professionalism, and Malpractice Issues in Estate Planning and Administration," *American Law Institute–American Bar Association Course of Study* 75 (1998): 67.
27. Patrick J. Schiltz, "Legal Ethics in Decline, The Elite Law Firm, The Elite Law School, and the Moral Formation at the Novice Attorney," Minnesota Law Review 82 (February 1998): 705, 747.
28. Ibid., 747.
29. Thomas F. Bergin, The Law Teacher: A Man Divided against Himself," *Virginia Law Review* 54 (1968): 637, 638.
30. The *U.S. News & World Report* law school rankings, which place law schools in one of four tiers, has accelerated this process, with deans pushing their faculties to publish more articles. Faculty productivity arguably translates into more public recognition, a factor reflected in the importance placed on "reputation" in the *U.S. News* rankings. *U.S. News* would argue that ranking law schools is good for prospective law students, giving them much needed information. The irony is that the *U.S. News* rankings have driven law school administrations to reward time spent publishing rather than time spent improving the quality of the classroom experience. Publishing presumably has more impact on the school's overall reputation. Quality of teaching does not translate nearly as readily into industry-wide recognition. This shift in incentives imposes an immediate cost on law students and their educational experience.
31. Schiltz, "Legal Ethics in Decline," 750–52.
32. Marin R. Scordato, "The Dualist Model of Legal Teaching and Scholarship," *American University Law Review* 40 (Fall 1990): 367. See also Deborah L. Rhode, *In the Interests of Justice: Reforming the Legal Profession*, (Oxford: Oxford University Press, 2001), 185–206, proposing a variety of approaches to legal education reform.
33. Schiltz, "Legal Ethics in Decline," 756. See also Mary Ann Glendon, *A Nation Under Lawyers*, (Cambridge: Harvard University Press, 1994), Chapters 10 and 11, for an excellent critique of modern legal education.
34. Ramos, "Legal and Law School Malpractice," 910, 911.
35. Ramos, "Legal and Law School Malpractice," 913–14, 914–15, 912.
36. Geoffrey C. Hazard, "Ethical Opportunity in the Practice of Law," *San Diego Law Review* 27 (1990), 127, 135.
37. Pearce, "Teaching Ethics Seriously," 728–29.
38. Marcia Chambers, "Why Lawyers Must Police Themselves," *National Law Journal*, 11 November 1991.
39. Joshua S. Rubenstein, "Compensation of Attorney/Executors," *New York Law Journal*, 29 April 1996.
40. Armstrong, "Lawyers Go after Own."
41. Ibid.

Chapter 8
An Inadequate Safety Net

1. This account is taken from Bill McKelway, "Victims Litter Tale of 2 Lives Led by Lawyer," *Richmond Times-Dispatch*, 29 March 1992.

2. J. P. Sherwood, "Va. Lawyer's Tangled Legacy: $41 Million Owed Clients, Investors," *Washington Post*, 29 March 1992; McKelway, "Victims Litter Tale."
3. Sherwood, "Va. Lawyer's Tangled Legacy."
4. McKelway, "Victims Litter Tale."
5. Ibid.
6. Joe Cosco, "Murray's Son Pleads Guilty to Embezzling $126,000," *Virginian-Pilot and Ledger-Star*, 7 August 1993.
7. Sherwood, "Va. Lawyer's Tangled Legacy."
8. McKelway, "Victims Litter Tale."
9. Sherwood, "Va. Lawyer's Tangled Legacy."
10. Ibid.
11. McKelway, "Victims Litter Tale."
12. Ibid.
13. Ibid.
14. Sherwood, "Va. Lawyer's Tangled Legacy."
15. McKelway, "Victims Litter Tale."
16. "Lawmakers to Examine Way Estates Are Handled," UPI (Regional News), 20 July 1992.
17. Bob Evans and Ken Armstrong, "Lawyer's Misdeeds Long Went Ignored; Bar Record Spotless Up To Day of Suicide," Arizona Republic, 26 November 1992.
18. "Wife Says She Had No Knowledge of Husband's Schemes," *U.P.I.*, 1 April 1992; Cosco, "Murray's Son Pleads Guilty."
19. *Burcher v. McCauley*, 871 FSupp. (ED Va 1994), 864–65.
20. Ibid., 870.
21. Alan Cooper, "Virginia Bar Tries to Focus," *National Law Journal*, 18 January 1993.
22. Virginia State Bar, Special Committee on Lawyers Serving as Fiduciaries, "Recommendations in Favor of a Program of Random Reviews," report to the Council of the Virginia State Bar, Richmond, 1993, 11.
23. Ibid., 13.
24. Ibid., 16, 13.
25. Cooper, "Virginia Bar Tries to Focus."
26. Jon Frank, "Murray Land Is Auctioned in Scandal's Wake," *Virginian-Pilot and Ledger-Star*, 4 March 1993.
27. Cooper, "Virginia Bar Tries to Focus."
28. Manuel R. Ramos, "Legal Malpractice: Reforming Lawyers and Law Professors," *Tulane Law Review* 70 (1996): 2583, 2587.
29. Jeffrey Good, "Forgotten Victims, Perspective," *St. Petersburg Times*, 11 September 1994.
30. ABA Section on Real Property, Probate & Trust Law, "Principles for Attorneys Acting in Other Fiduciary Roles," (16 October 1992), cited in Bradley R. Cook, "Principles for Attorneys Acting in Other Fiduciary Roles," *Property and Probate* 6 (March/April 1992): 6.
31. Patricia Gormely Prince and Randall J. Soverinsky, "Probate and Estate Planning: How to Protect the 'Protected Person,'" *Michigan Bar Journal* 75 (December 1996): 1296, 1299.
32. See Molly McDonough, "The Push for Mandatory Coverage: Illinois Bar Wants to Make Malpractice the Law," *ABA Journal eReport*, 11 January 2002.
33. The Ohio Supreme Court recently adopted rules mandating that lawyers at least reveal that they do not have such coverage. Alaska and South Dakota also have such rules, and Virginia lawyers must certify annually whether they have such coverage. *U.S. Law Week* 69, no. 45 (29 May 2001).
34. Manuel R. Ramos, "Legal Malpractice: Reforming Lawyers and Law Professors," *Tulane Law Review* 70 (1996): 2583.
35. Ibid., 2618–20.
36. Note that many other countries mandate minimum limits for professional liability insurance as a condition of practicing law in those countries. According to studies conducted in 1995, England, France, Germany, Australia, Belgium, the Netherlands, Sweden, British Columbia, Ontario, and Quebec are among the countries and Canadian provinces that require some form of malpractice insurance. Albert Rogers et al. eds., *Liability of Lawyers and Indemnity Insurance* (London: Kluwer, 1995).
37. Thomas G. Bousquet, "It's Time for Mandatory Malpractice Insurance," *Texas Lawyer*, 6 December 1993, 17.
38. Ramos, "Legal Malpractice," 2612 n. 138, citing Harry N. Schneider, "At Issue: Mandatory Insurance, Not an

Invitation to Frivolous Suits," *ABA Journal* 79 (November 1993): 104.
39. Ibid., 2609–10.
40. Ibid., 2611.
41. This burdensome debt limit was recently documented by the Nellie Mae Corporation (the largest provider of student loans), which found that "lawyers who have been out of school between one and three years . . . had an average education-related debt of $52,600." Mark Hansen, "And Debt's All, Folks: To New Lawyers Paying Off Student Loans, 'Budget' Is Not a Bad Word," *ABA Journal* 85 (June 1999): 24.
42. Consumers are turning to the innovative use of consumer protection statutes as another remedy for lawyers who have damaged them. New Jersey, Louisiana, Massachusetts, Oregon, and Texas are states that "have found that deceptive practice and consumer fraud statutes apply to professionals." Paul Marcotte, "New Threat to Attorneys? N.J. Court: Lawyers Liable for Consumer Fraud," *ABA Journal* 74 (December 1988): 18.
43. Ramos, "Legal Malpractice," 2601 n. 85, citing Geoffrey C. Hazard, "Ethics," *National Law Journal*, 6 July 1992.
44. Ibid., citing Deborah L. Rhode, "Institutionalizing Ethics," *Case Western Reserve Law Review* 44 (1994): 665, 697.
45. In a recent *ABA Journal eReport* it was noted that the ABA seemed to be following this trend. "At the annual meeting in August, the Standing Committee on Client Protection will recommend to the House of Delegates that the Model Rules of Professional Conduct be amended to require lawyers to make a disclosure if they are not covered by insurance." The article quotes Illinois State Bar Association president Tim Eaton of Chicago who thinks that disclosure is not enough. "It still puts the client at risk. . . . The client may not understand the gravity of the situation if they are harmed or need some type of protection." *ABA Journal eReport*, 11 January 2002.
46. "Bar Fund May Help Some Involved in Lawyer Swindle," UPI Regional News, 12 March 1992.
47. Harriet L. Turney and John A. Holtaway, "Client Protection Funds—Lawyers Put Their Money Where Their Mouths Are," *Professional Lawyer* 9 (February 1998): 18, 19.
48. Ibid., 18.
49. "Bar Fund May Help."
50. Frederick Miller, "If You Can't Trust Your Lawyer . . . ?" *University of Pennsylvania Law Review* 138 (January 1990): 785, 791.
51. "The American Bar Association Model Code of Professional Responsibility," Canon 9, Ethical Consideration 7, in John S. Dzienkowski, ed., *Professional Responsibility Standards Rules & Statutes*, 1998–99 ed. (St. Paul: West Group, 1998).
52. Turney and Holtaway, "Client Protection Funds," 18.
53. Ibid.
54. Elaine Song, "Lawyers Who Steal: Rich Man, Poor Man, Beggar Man, Thief, Doctor, Lawyer," *Connecticut Law Tribune*, 23 October 1995.
55. Ibid.
56. Good, "Forgotten Victims, Perspective."
57. Turney and Holtaway, "Client Protection Funds," 19.
58. Ibid.
59. Joshua S. Rubenstein, "Compensation of Attorney/Executors," *New York Law Journal*, 29 April 1996.

Chapter 9
A Failure of Character or Discipline?

1. Deborah L. Rhode, "Moral Character as a Professional Credential," *Yale Law Journal* 94 (1985): 491, 520.
2. As reviewed by Paul Reidinger, "Tempering the Crassness: Ethical Values Need to Re-Enter the Mix for Lawyers Stuck on the Bottom Line," *ABA Journal* 85 (June 1999): 84.
3. Patrick J. Schiltz, "Legal Ethics in Decline: The Elite Law Firm, the Elite Law School, and the Moral Formation of the Novice Attorney," *Minnesota Law Review* 82 (February 1988): 705.
4. Richard Brust, "Recent Rise of Client Escrow Thefts Points to 'Peter-to-Paul'

Syndrome: Tight Economy, Flood of Lawyers Seen as Causes," *The Legal Intelligencer*, Suburban Edition, 7 May 1997.

5. Ibid.
6. See, for example, the story of Pittsburgh lawyer Charles Thorp detailed in the *Wall Street Journal*. Gregory Stricharchuk, "Hooked on Options: Compulsive Trading Brings Down Lawyer Who Used Client Cash," *Wall Street Journal*, 18 April 1990. In a letter from Thorp's attorney, Lawrence O'Toole, to the Disciplinary Counsel of the Pennsylvania Bar Association, 7 June 1989, (on file with Office of disciplinary counsel, 1010 Manor Complex, 564 Forbes Avenue, Pittsburgh, PA 15219), Thorp's lawyer blames his thefts from estates and trusts in his fiduciary on a compulsive addiction to playing the stock market.
7. Tricia S. Heil, "The Texas Bar—Getting In and Staying In: Chemical Dependency and Mental Health Issues in Texas Licensing and Disciplinary Procedures," *Texas Bar Journal* 61 (March 1988): 266, 267.
8. Ibid., 267.
9. Rick B. Allan, "Alcoholism, Drug Abuse and Lawyers: Are We Ready to Address the Denial?" *Creighton Law Review* 31 (December 1991): 265, 273.
10. Dianne Molvig, "WISLAP Combats Career Killers," *Wisconsin Lawyer* 71 (May 1998): 14, 16.
11. "Lawyers Concerned for Lawyers," descriptive Brochure Available from Massachusetts Lawyer's Assistance Program, 7 Marshall Street, Boston, MA 02108.
12. Allan, "Alcoholism, Drug Abuse and Lawyers," 268.
13. Elizabeth Cohen,"Who Needs to Know?: When Reporting Lawyer Misconduct, Just Telling the Judge Isn't Enough,"*ABA Journal* 85 (April 1999): 77.
14. Allan, "Alcoholism, Drug Abuse and Lawyers," 269, 266.
15. Ibid., 265–66.
16. Ibid., 273.
17. Ibid., 268.
18. *In re Kersey*, 520 A2d 321 (1987), 328.
19. Jeffrey N. Pennell, "Ethics, Professionalism, and Malpractice Issues in Estate Planning and Administration," *American Law Institute–American Bar Association Course of Study* 75 (1988): 67, 184.
20. Manuel R. Ramos, "Legal Malpractice: The Profession's Dirty Little Secret," Vanderbilt Law Review 47 (1994): 1657, 1750 n. 196, citing Kay Ostberg and Theresa Meehan Rudy, *If You Want to Sue a Lawyer . . . A Directory of Legal Malpractice Attorneys* (New York: Random House, 1991): 11.
21. See Deborah L. Rhode, "Symposium: The Future of the Legal Profession: Institutionalizing Ethics," *Case Western Reserve Law Review* 44 (1994): 665, 695–96.
22. Mary M. Devlin, "The Development of Lawyer Disciplinary Procedures in the United States," *Georgetown Journal of Legal Ethics* 7 (1994): 911, 912.
23. Ibid., 919–20.
24. Ibid., 921.
25. Ibid., 927.
26. Ibid., 930–31.
27. Ibid., 933–34.
28. Jane Ruffin, "Many Lawyers Who Embezzle Not Prosecuted," Raleigh *News Observer*, 8 December 1991.
29. Christine Stapleton, "Pinellas Prosecutor Cuts Colleagues No Slack," *Palm Beach Post*, 26 February 1994.
30. Tracy Breton, "Penalties Vary Widely for Lawyers Who Steal," *Providence Sunday Journal*, 16 February 1997.
31. Ramos, "Legal Malpractice," 1697.
32. Breton, "Penalties Vary Widely."
33. Jeffrey Good, "She Paid For Her Crimes—Didn't She?" *St. Petersburg Times*, 26 March 1995.
34. *State of Florida v. Lauren Ann Sill*, Case #93–05819 CFANO, Criminal Court File (Circuit Court, Pinellas County), letter of Gary A. Soracchi, Probation & Parole Services, 26 March 1997.

Chapter 10
Probate in the Twenty-First Century

1. National College of Probate Judges Home Page, www.ncpj.org.
2. The description of the changes in New Hampshire probate procedures and courts was given by Judge John Maher,

chief administrative judge of the New Hampshire Probate Court and president of the National College of Probate Judges, telephone interview, 27 March 2000; interview, Baltimore, Md., 31 March 2000.

3. See New Hampshire Statutes Annotated RSA §554:1-a, which, after amendments in 1998 and 1999, now provides "Notwithstanding any provision of law, whenever a deceased dies testate and the surviving spouse, or if no spouse, an only child is named in the will as the sole beneficiary of the deceased's estate and is appointed to serve as fiduciary; or whenever a deceased dies intestate and the surviving spouse or, if no spouse, an only child is the sole heir of the deceased's estate and is appointed to serve as fiduciary, there shall be no requirement for an inventory of the estate, no requirement for a bond, and no requirement for an accounting of assets. Administration of the estate shall be completed upon the fiduciary's filing, and the probate court's approval of an affidavit of administration."
4. While reforms can minimize the risk, they can never eliminate it completely. Following the Fairbanks case, the New Hampshire House Judiciary and Family Law Committee heard testimony about the case of attorney Charles E. Chretien who also took money from client estates and trusts. In an article describing Judge John Maher's testimony before the committee, Maher indicated that because of the Fairbanks case, Chretien's clients would have increased hope of compensation due to the new policies requiring bonds in most probate cases and that "'to say this is shades of Fairbanks' is just not true . . . because Fairbanks stole millions of dollars while Chretien took thousands." Maher and Judge Raymond Cloutier, who supervised Chretien's cases, also noted "the efficiency of a computer system that has, since 1994, alerted judges and probate registers when administrators of estates and trusts do not file the accountings required by law." But they warned that there may be "land mines" and "ticking time bombs" of wrongdoing in the paper files of older cases that have been inactive for several years. Roger Talbot, "Judge Never Suspected Thefts," *Manchester Union Leader*, 18 May 1997.
5. *Schware v. Board of Bar Examiners of the State of New Mexico*, 353 US 232 (1957), 247 (J. Frankfurter, concurring).

Glossary

▼

Administration: Collecting, managing, and distributing the estate of a deceased person or "decedent." This is done by a court-appointed representative known as the "administrator" or the "executor."

Administrator: The person or institution named by the probate court to collect, manage, and distribute the estate when a decedent either dies without a will ("intestate") or does not name someone in his or her will to take on this task.

Attestation: The dual act of watching the testator of a will sign the will and then writing one's signature as a witness.

Beneficiary: The person who is to benefit from the income or principal of a trust or the person named to receive a bequest under a will

Codicil: A document that modifies or amends a will and that is executed with the same formalities, including proper witnesses, as a will.

Conservator: The person or institution appointed by a probate court to manage the affairs of a person who is incapacitated. If the conservator is merely appointed to manage the financial affairs of the incapacitated person, this is known as a "conservator of the estate." If the conservator is to be accountable for the physical well-being and care of the incapacitated adult, this is known as a "conservator of the person." In many states, this function is also known as a "guardian of the estate" or a "guardian of the person."

Escheat: The general principle under most state inheritance laws that provides for an intestate decedent's estate to pass to the state when there are no heirs to inherit the property.

Execution: The act of putting one's signature on a will. Also the actual implementation of the provisions of a will.

Executor: The person or institution named or "nominated" by the testator of a will and appointed by the probate court to implement its provisions.

Fiduciary: In the probate area, someone who is appointed by the court to act in the best interests of another. For example, executors, administrators, trustees, and guardians are all fiduciaries who owe a legal duty to those for whom they manage property, and their breach of such duty is actionable.

Grantor: The person who creates a trust. Synonymous with the terms "donor," "settlor," or "trustor" in relation to a trust.

Guardian: The person or institution named or "nominated" by the testator of a will to assume responsibility for the testator's minor children. Also, the person or institution appointed by the probate court to act on behalf of an incapacitated adult. (See also "conservator.")

Guardian ad Litem: The person appointed by the probate court for the limited purpose of representing a minor child or unborn beneficiary's legal interests in the context of a legal proceeding. Unlike a "guardian," a guardian ad litem (typically an attorney) has no power to make decisions about the minor child's physical custody or financial assets.

Heirs: Those relatives who are legally entitled under state law to inherit the estate of a person who dies without a will or "intestate."

Inter vivos trust: A trust created during the grantor's lifetime (as opposed to a "testatmentary trust" created at the time of death, under the terms of a will). Also known as a "living trust."

Intestacy: Having died without a will.

Intestacy statutes: State laws defining who is legally entitled to inherit a decedent's estate if that decedent dies without a will.

Issue: The lineal descendants of a person, including children, grandchildren, and great-grandchildren.

Joint tenancy: The form of title to property that provides for co-ownership and which results in title to the property passing automatically to the surviving joint tenants when one co-owner dies, by "right of survivorship." The property passes outside of the probate process. To be distinguished from a "tenancy in common," which results in a co-owner's interest in the property being transferred by will or by intestacy statutes.

Letter of administration or letters testamentary: Official appointment papers signed by the probate court so that an administrator or executor may demonstrate they have the legal authority to manage, sell, or distribute the decedent's property.

Marshaling assets: The act of identifying and inventorying the decedent's assets in an estate. A legal duty of the administrator or executor.

Personal representative: The umbrella term used by some states and the Uniform Probate Code to designate either an administrator or an executor.

Power of appointment: A provision in a will or similar document that grants an individual (known as the "donee") the power to direct trust assets at termination of the trust to himself, his estate, or another individual or group named in the will or similar document.

Power of attorney: A document that grants authority to act on one's behalf to another (known as the "attorney-in-fact") creating an agency relationship between the two. The grantor of the power is the principal and the grantee is the agent. A "durable" power of attorney is one that survives the incapacity of the principal. Such agents may perform a variety of functions on behalf of the principal including buying, selling, and managing property.

Probate: The process of validating a will, if one exists, and administering a deceased person's estate.

Probate asset or probate estate: Property that passes under a will or by intestacy, in contrast to property that passes automatically, outside the probate process, like jointly held property and contractual assets such as life insurance.

Probate court: The court in each state that oversees the collection, management, and distribution of decedents' estates. Also known as "surrogate's court" or "orphan's court" in some states.

Remainderman: An individual who is named in a trust to receive the principal or corpus when the trust comes to an end or "terminates." This is contrasted with an "income beneficiary" who is named to receive benefits from the trust during its ongoing existence.

Residuary estate: The assets that remain in an estate after the specific bequests have been made and any taxes and expenses of administration have been paid. The balance of the estate is also known as the residue or residual estate and is distributed under a "residuary clause" in a will.

Tenancy in common: A method of co-ownership between two or more persons under which the interest of a deceased co-owner passes in accordance with her will, or, if there is no will, in accordance with the laws of intestate succession.

Testamentary: This phrase denotes those matters having to do with a will. Wills become effective only upon the death of the testator who executes them, thus the phrase can also mean effective upon death.

Testamentary capacity: The requirement that a person making a will (1) understand that she is making a permanent disposition of her estate, (2) understand the extent of her assets, and (3) is aware of which people constitute the "natural objects of her bounty," in other words, her relatives. All three must be present for the testator to create a valid will.

Testamentary trust: A trust created by the terms of a will. Such a trust comes into existence when the testator dies, as contrasted with an inter vivos trust, which comes into existence during the grantor's life.

Testacy: Having died with a will.

Testator: The individual who makes or "executes" a will is the testator. If one dies with a will one is said to have died "testate."

Trustee: The person or institution designated by the grantor of a trust or appointed by the court to assume the fiduciary duty of holding and administering a trust for the beneficiaries.

Uniform Probate and Trust Codes: Model probate and trust statutes promulgated by the National Conference of Commissioners on Uniform State Laws and adopted in whole or in part by many states.

Index

▼